My Life On

Best wishes

Capt. John

A Southwest Florida native, Captain John Morgan reminisces about
his life of fishing, boat building and adventure.

My Life On The Water

Capt. John Morgan

On the cover is a 41x14 foot sport fishing boat that I designed and built while in the business I founded when I started my adventure in fiberglass.

ISBN : 1-4196-1546-7

To order additional copies, please contact us.
BookSurge, LLC
www.booksurge.com
1-866-308-6235
orders@booksurge.com

My Life On The Water

If you were to draw a straight line from the beginning of this man's life, to the retirement years of old age, all you would find, would be boats, and friends. If he has ever met you, he considers he has met a friend. You would have to include all the waterways of the U.S.A. and the Bahama Islands as being part of him. Just simply, this is his life and how he lived it. Also, how he loved every minute of this way, (his way).

His life "mate"

RACHEL

PREFACE

Collecting my thoughts, of friends, boats and places, I'm enjoying my past even now. I'm just going to make my retirement days another adventure for this time in my life, sitting on the patio in my easy chair. I just cruised through waves of memories, and decided to jot them down. Since retiring, it's certainly not a dull path for me. Boating, boat building cattle ranches, and orange groves could sum up the most of my life as a true Florida native. I am not writing this book for money or fame, or trying to look like a hero, because I know that I am only like a grain of sand on a huge beach, and I hope the readers can get some enjoyment out of my experiences of this travel through my life.

I dedicate this book to my family who have been by my side through thick and thin and have never let me down. Also, to my Pastor Grant Thigpen of New Hope Ministries, who never gave up on me during some real rough times.

CHAPTER ONE

Being born about the time the "Big Depression" started was probably not a great time for me to come into this world. I was born Aug 26, 1929 in Fort Myers, Florida, at Jack and Lilly Collier's house on the corner of Monroe St. and Victoria Ave. You could probably say I "hit the ground running," as my wandering ways started early in life!

Boating and boat building had to be first in my life from the very beginning. For the most of my time now, it is still close to first! This is me.

My mother was Mae Collier, born on Marco Island, Florida; my dad was, C.C. "Pat" Morgan, Jr., born in Fort Ogden, Florida.

Grandpa C.C. Morgan, Sr. was a judge in Desoto County. He decided my dad should go to college, so he sent him off to Riverside Military Academy in Georgia. When dad finished the Academy, he and my mother were married. They had met when dad was on a survey team, surveying the road from Fort Myers to Marco Island. That was 41 to Naples, to Belle Meade, to a ferry crossing at Bear Point. The new Marco Bridge crosses there now.

I never got to know Grandma Morgan; she died before I was old enough to remember her. She was a Mizell from the Fort Ogden area. She had two brothers, Floyd and Everett Mizell. Uncle Floyd had two sons, Kenneth and David. They all had huge orange groves and cattle ranches.

Every summer my dad would take me to Fort Ogden to visit them and go on their cattle round up. Following dad around and watching the cattle branding, was a great adventure for me.

Bone Mizell was a first cousin to my grand mother Morgan. There is a large marker at Zolfo Springs Pioneer Park dubbing him "Desoto County's Wag Cowboy." Lots of books and stories are written and told about him, mostly true. He seemed to have this habit of cattle rustling, for others and himself.

One time, caught rustling cattle for himself, he was taken in to court for trial. Standing before the Judge he said, "I don't understand this, as long as I was rustling for the ranch I worked on, it was OK to do this. Since I rustled a few for myself, it's wrong." The Judge said, "I have to send you to prison." They took him to prison, fed him lunch, and took him home. The sentence was served.

Near the Mizell ranch was the Hudson ranch. Dad and I would go with them on their round up's too. That's when I learned to eat rice and tomato gravy, cooked outside in a large cast iron pot. That was good eating! I have made it lots of times since then for my own children, and they think it's great too!

After all the ranching, my dad started running a tugboat for the Gulf Oil Company. This one trip with him was when Gulf Oil had a contract to deliver all the asphalt to Captiva Island, to surface the road from Captiva to Sanibel. He would push the barge into Blind Pass channel up to a dock on Captiva. We had to start in about half tide, with a rising tide, because the water was real shallow across the grass flats. He would push the barge in until the tug ran aground.

The mate on the tug was a cousin of mine, George Daniels. After the barge and tug was tied up to the dock, we had a 10 foot row boat we carried along with us. My dad, George, and I would take off in it to gather clams, and scallops.

We discovered a little cove full of clams, but found we had this one problem. There was a big house on the shoreline and the owner claimed rights to the clams. George was a tall man, and he would get in the water beside the boat, with dad and I pretending we were fishing. George would be digging clams, and I guess we were lucky, we never got caught. George sure made some good clam chowder.

Going up and down the river with my dad on the tugboat, pushing barges, and digging clams, was a really exciting time in my life. This is probably the beginning of my life long desires to be on the water.

About this time World War II had started, and Dad went down to join the Navy. He found he had a serious heart condition. When he was a baby he had rheumatic fever that left him with a leakage of the heart, so he didn't pass the physical.

Soon after this, when I was about 12 years old, on our front porch, me on the steps and him in the swing, he just fell over dead. That was a very sad time for me.

My mom and sister, Shirley, and I had to move across the street with Mom's parents, Jack and Lilly Collier.

Mom went to work for the Coca Cola bottling plant and granddad

Jack went to work for Fort Myers Shipbuilding. They were building barges for the army at that time.

I got a job at the bowling alley setting up pins, working till about midnight every night. I made about a dollar and fifty cents a night. Soldiers would come in from Page field and Buckingham air bases and get drunk. They would throw the balls halfway down the alley before they landed and rolled to the pins. The later it got, the drunker they got, the more dangerous it became for me. They would throw the balls before I could get all the pins set up. I had to scramble out of the way, as pins were flying everywhere. They did have their fun!

Also at that time, I had a paper route starting at five a.m. At the end of the route I rushed to school, which is part of the day I didn't like to well. I liked the outdoors better. I saved most of my money up from those two jobs.

Grandma Lilly took over raising me, as my mother worked most of the time.

My mother had two sisters, Elizabeth and Fay, and one brother Bruce. Elizabeth married Jack Malloy. Fay married Hugh Mauck and Bruce married Lois Barwick. They all had two kids each; my mom had me, then Shirley. Elizabeth had Betty Joe and Jimmy, Fay had Helen and Libby, and Bruce had Robert Bruce and Tommy. We all lived in Fort Myers at that time, as the original Collier families had left Marco Island in about 1926.

Captain Jack Collier and John Cawley Morgan

CHAPTER TWO

When my Collier family left New Smyrna, they were aboard the schooner *Robert E. Lee*. It was built by my great grandfather W.T. Collier, up on the St. Johns River.

Arriving at Marco Island, they bought out a few squatters, and became the first real settlers on Marco Island. Collier City, just inside Caxambas Pass was named after them.

Grandpa Jack Collier married Lilly Josephine Daniels. She was born at Lostman's River. Her mother was Sally Weeks, daughter of John Weeks. Family tradition says her mother was an Indian. I don't know if it was Seminole or Creek. Her sister was the mother of the Hamilton's who lived at Lostman's River at that time.

Sally married Jim Daniels while they lived at Lostman's River. Later on they moved to Marco Island so their children could go to school. Lostman's River is about halfway between Everglades City and Shark River, and is now part of Everglades National Park.

Grandpa Jack was born in New Smyrna, Florida, into a family of sailors and boat builders. After sailing around to Marco Island, they started building sailing schooners, from 1870 to the early 1900's. They built approximately 20 boats, up to 65 foot in length. They engaged in trading, between Key West and New Orleans, Louisiana. At that time, one of the first schooners built was for the Key West Harbor Pilots. They used it to bring in bigger ships through the channel.

Another schooner built, named the *Speedwell*, was taken on her maiden voyage, to Key West by Captain Bill Collier. Then came up a fast hard squall. Captain Bill had his three sons and some passengers on board with him, and a preacher. With his three sons and the passengers in the cabin, he told the preacher to drop the mainsail. The wind was really blowing hard by then. Instead of dropping the mainsail he fell on his knees and started praying. The squall hit harder and capsized the boat. The sons and passengers were trapped in the cabin and drowned. Captain Bill and the preacher held on to the keel of the boat. Another boat came along and rescued them. This turned Captain Bill into an atheist. He said, "If there is a God, he would not have let this happen."

Captain Bill turned all of his skills into money making. He invented and built the clam dredge, with the help of his brothers. He later sold the dredge to the clam factory that was built on the Collier property.

My Granddad Jack owned two schooners, the *Eureka* and the *Falcon*. The *Eureka* was a 65 foot schooner they built on Marco. The *Falcon* was a smaller schooner they purchased up in Mississippi. She was 45 feet long, then cut in to and lengthened to 55 feet.

This one story of Granddad's, I remember well. He started to Key West with the *Eureka* loaded with farm products, and fish, and started watching the barometer going very low. They had no way in those days to know that a hurricane was coming. It kept blowing harder and harder. As he sighted Key West, the wind had blown all of the sails off, and they were under bare poles. When they entered the harbor, he dropped anchor. The anchor started dragging and the *Eureka* got sandwiched in between two larger ships.

Both of Granddad's crew members jumped off onto the larger ships. The *Eureka* kept on dragging anchor in towards the wharf. As soon as she was clear of the two ships that had sandwiched her in, they started yelling for him to come back for them, but he could not get back.

The *Eureka* dragged its anchor until her transom was up against the sea wall and a dock along side her. Granddad was able to get off and tie her off from the sea wall. He went up to the post office to wait out the storm, which at that time was the federal building. This was the 1910 hurricane. At 120 miles per hour it blew the weather instruments down, and then he said it really started blowing.

They weathered the storm out, and the next morning he didn't know whether he had a boat left or not. He went down to the dock and the old *Eureka* had made it through all right. He spent about a week patching up sails, gathering up another crew, and then sailing back to Marco.

Another story Granddad told me was about his brothers being in a storm on the schooner "*Guide*." Leaving New Orleans, his brothers, W.D. and B.F. were bound for Fort Myers with cargo. A strong breeze sprang up from the south west. The next morning the wind shifted to the west, and increasing to gale force strength, about 25 miles southwest of Cedar Keys, a breaker hit from the starboard side, washing W.D. and B.F. overboard. W.D. grabbed the tiller rope and pulled himself back on board. B. F. was seen swimming to the small boat they had launched. He was in their sight about 20 minutes. The gale continued all night, and then all hope of saving him was given up. So they set their course for Fort Myers.

There have been a lot of books and stories about my families while they lived on Marco Island, some true, some changed. The most I know is, they strived to make a "new beginning" for every one there.

The schooner *Eureka* was built in 1898 by the Collier brothers on Marco Island Florida. She was skippered by my Granddad Captain Jack Collier, one of the youngest Collier Brothers. Her dimensions were: length 65 foot, beam 18 foot, draft 4 foot. Her frames were natural crooks from Maderia, (Florida Mahogany). Her planking was Georgia pine. By natural crooks we mean tree limbs that are contoured to the hull sides and bottom. She was built for the coastal trade between Key West and New Orleans, Louisiana. Her cargo would be mostly fish and produce such as pineapples, tomatoes, etc. On her return trips she would be loaded with canned goods, hardware, furniture and sometimes passengers.

The railroad came in, and there was no more need for the sail boats. The *Eureka* was sold to Captain Ferguson Hall, an old friend of the family. Captain Ferg installed a 75 horse power diesel engine in the *Eureka*, and made several trips with her to Cuba and Honduras, bringing back crocodile hides and mahogany lumber. He modified her sailing rig by taking off her topmast and cutting off her bowsprit. He claimed she had too much sail area for the Caribbean, as it blows much harder and the seas are much bigger down there. The *Eureka* once more became active between Fort Myers and Key West, towing barges to Key West for the Army during World War II. The barges were built by Fort Myers Ship Building Company.

By the end of the war the *Eureka* was sold to some Cubans. They took her down to Cuba and started a freight business down there. Soon after that, she was wrecked on a reef just off the Cuban coast. The *Eureka* had a long and fruitful life of approximately 50 years. She was still a strong and sound vessel when she came to her death on that coral reef.

The original *Eureka*

This is the *Eureka* after Capt. Ferg modified her sailing rig

CHAPTER THREE

Boat building, and my trips down the Caloosahatchee River, started when I was about 10 years old. Just before my dad passed away, I built a 6 ½ foot sailboat in our back yard. I knew then that I was born to build boats!

When I was about 15 years old, I built a 16 foot sailboat with the help of my granddad, and two best friends George Messer and Bobby Ireland. Both friends lived near me and we had some great experiences with that boat sailing around together. Almost every weekend we would go down to Shell Island, which is at the mouth of the Caloosahatchee River, and gather oysters, or on down to Captiva Island to dig clams, depending on how much time we had, and which way the wind was blowing.

At this time the Cubans had these big sailing smacks, and they fished for grouper off Sanibel and Captiva. When there was a storm or a hurricane coming they would come in and anchor up under Sanibel Island.. They could ride out a hurricane here in fairly calm water. In this one particular hurricane, a Cuban smack broke anchor and drug in on some big grass flats, just off Punta Rassa, in the mouth of the Caloosahatchee River. She went in on high water during the hurricane, and when the wind switched, she was aground. This smack drew about 6 or 7 feet of water, but you could wade all around her. We used to go down and go aboard her, just to look around.

After a couple weeks they sent a tug up from Havana with another smack. She was a big one, about 85 or 90 feet long, with an auxiliary diesel engine in her. They anchored up right off Punta Rassa. She was the mother ship to the tug and her crew. They took anchors and bridled out behind the tugboat, and ran the engine. The propeller wash dug a ditch all the way to the Smack. It floated her off. While the mother ship was there, we would go and stay with them overnight. We became really good friends with the cook, as he would stay there to prepare meals for the crew, while they were working at getting the other smack off the sand bar. Another friend of mine, Gene Lamb, was taking Spanish in high school, and got to where we could talk to the cook pretty well. He insisted we stay and eat with them.

On these Cuban smacks they had big live wells where they keep the grouper and other fish, and turtles, alive so they could take them back to Havana. This cook would dive into the live well, and catch a turtle and butcher him for dinner. He also made some kind of fritters that you dipped in syrup. They were really delicious.

They finally got the smaller smack off, and they all headed back to Havana. I was sorry to see them go.

Another trip I remember, Bobby Ireland, and George Messer, and I took off one Friday and sailed down to Fort Myers Beach, arriving about midnight. This was during the war, and there was a big gunnery school at Fort Myers. Soldiers patrolled the beaches. We anchored the boat right off the beach, got our blankets and waded ashore and slept on the beach. About the time I was falling asleep, I felt something poking me in the back. I looked around and it was a soldier with a rifle. They thought we were German spies that had come ashore from a submarine. We hung around there until about noon the next day, and then sailed back to Fort Myers.

With all of these trips my friends and I were taking, I didn't always tell my mom I was leaving. She told everyone, "Since he always comes back safe, I won't bother to worry about him anymore."

Uncle Jack Maloy said, "I'm going with that boy on the boat to see where he goes, and why." We slept on the boat every night, gathered clams and oysters, ate some raw and cooked some. He had a great time and told mom, "I know why John stays down the river so much, I didn't want to come home myself."

My paper route went right by the Thomas Edison Home. One morning just about daylight, I decided to go in and take a look around, discovered a swimming pool, so I decided to take a swim. From then on for the next few weeks, I made this a regular stop. Several years later I saw a man that told me he was care taker for the Edison Home, and he lived in a little cottage right beside the pool. I used to wake him up with my swimming. He had been watching me all the time and I didn't know it.

One Christmas vacation George, Bobby, and I decided to sail down to Marco Island, and spend a few days there. George had lived there some years before. The weather was really nice as we were sailing down. We visited around with some of George's relatives. We had a perfect sail all the way back home.

There was a little island on the north end of Sanibel, called

Mysterious Island. An old hermit lived there, but we had never been inside there. One night we were on our way to Captiva to dig clams, and it started blowing real hard out of the north, so we sailed into a little inlet between two of the little islands, off the north end of Sanibel. The next morning the tide had fallen, and we were aground. So we went overboard to pull the boat into deeper water, and found we were on a clam bar, and picked up all of them we could. By then the tide had risen enough to float the boat, so we went on through a little cut between the islands, and found a dock and a Seminole log canoe.

Up on the island there was an old house. We had found Mysterious Island by mistake. We didn't know whether to try to get out of there, or what to do. About that time the hermit came out on the dock, and invited us to come ashore and look around. He turned out to be a nice old man. He caught a black grouper off his dock and made us fish chowder. It was delicious. He told us to take the log canoe and go exploring through the islands. We spent the night with him, very glad to get out of the mosquitoes. We made several trips back to visit the old man. A couple years later I heard he had died.

Bobby and I were at the Gulf oil docks messing around with the sailboat, and he fell overboard. The river was full of jelly fish and when he came up he had one on top of his head. They were round and had like a 4 leaf clover on the top of them, with feelers hanging down. I thought he was a goner, because these feelers that hung down would sting the fire out of you. When we pulled him out, we started washing and peeling it off him. We saw he wasn't hurt, and it got funny. It didn't seem to bother him, the jelly fish or us laughing.

Gene Lamb had a 14 foot sailboat. One weekend Bobby and I decided to go down to Captiva. Gene couldn't go, but he said, "Why don't you take my boat for a change?" She was a fast boat so we decided to take her. We put all of our camping gear together, and loaded on board.

We headed down river, and got a couple of miles when a plank came out of her, and she sank in just a couple of minutes, before we knew what was happening. She didn't go all the way down, just filled with water and laid over on her side. Then Bobby said, "What are we going to do now, John?"

I said, "It looks like we're in a real scrape now."

We were almost in the middle of the river. The boat had a spruce spar in her about 18 feet long, so I pulled it out and took all the sails and rigging off. I told Bobby I was going to take it and use it like a life vest, and swim ashore. I told him to stay with the boat. I started swimming on in, and got to where I could wade. I saw a crab boat coming and he was towing the sailboat. At that time, they did a lot of crabbing on the Caloosahatchee River, using 18 or 20 foot inboard boats. We were just east of the Edison home, and able to get her up on the beach, to pull her out. I called Gene and told him about it, he didn't seem to be too upset. I went ahead and repaired the bottom, and got her back to sailing again.

Soon after my river running days, my grandmother told my uncles (the Daniels brothers) I didn't want to do anything but build boats, so they hired me. I think I was about 16 years old then.

Uncle Frank took care of all the business and all of the repair work. Uncle Henry was the builder and took me under his wings. He was a great teacher, and I was a hard worker. He was the kind of person who would take time to show you something, and had a quizzical way of teaching you, and you remembered it. I knew a little bit about boat building, and had no problems learning more.

We built all of the hulls; put the deck on, and then the first coat of paint. Then the other crew would take over and put the engines in. If there were to be a cabin, that crew would put that on. I worked there about a year, and then things slowed down. It was about that time the war came to an end.

When I turned 16 years old, I went for my driver's license. I had learned to drive in my granddad's model T Ford.

Granddad loved going to work every day at Ft. Myers Ship Building. He always drove down Evans Ave., to Palm Beach Blvd., to the Ship Yard. Coming home one evening, he started to turn off Palm Beach onto Evans Ave. and a car hit him broadside. He got out of his car, looked around, and said, "I declare, I don't know why you hit me, I've been turning here 20 years." No body knew what to say to him then. He never drove again. But Uncle Jack Maloy bought a Model T Coupe, and I got to drive him around in it.

How special granddad made me feel, as best he could. We ate avocados, guavas, and mangos together a lot. Grandma had a time with him, as he would hide the avocados in his cloths drawers to ripen, and then forget them.

My uncle Hugh was in the Army and stationed in Texas. He sent for Aunt Fay and the children to go out there. She asked me if I could go with them and help drive. Her daughters were very young then. I think Helen was about 6 and Libby was 3 or 4.

There was at that time a 45 mph speed limit to conserve tires and gasoline. Aunt Fay had a 41 Ford. We left Fort Myers and 3 days later we were in Texas. Hugh had rented a house for them to live in, so I spent a couple days there, and then caught the bus back to Fort Myers.

Every time I changed buses, they would announce all service men on first. This would take all of the seats and I would wind up standing. I stood up the first 2 days, and then a nice lady that had a suitcase in the aisle, told me to sit down on it. This was a nice trip except for all the standing. I had the chance to see a lot of interesting country, and we were lucky not to have any flat tires or motor trouble on the way out there. I was glad to get back to Fort Myers.

This is *Scorpion*, the third sailboat I built

CHAPTER FOUR

Bill Kepler, owner of a Bahama sailboat that I had worked on, got me the job as deck hand on the *Nepenthe*. She was a 65 foot house boat, fixed up as a yacht. She towed a 28 foot cruiser and carried two 18 foot skiffs, on davits, on each side. An ex-sheriff of Lee County, Fred Roberts, was captain, and he really knew the country. Most fishing parties were three or four week charters. That was a real experience for me because I loved the sea and the outdoors and this was right up my line.

To begin our charters, the first night usually was at Coon Key, which is on the south end of Marco Island. The next day we would run down to Lostman's River and stay about a week there, fishing all of the back waters in that area. Then, depending on how long the charter was, we would go on down to Shark River and fish all of that country, sometimes even go up to the head of it.

Captain Fred took a liking to me, and told me I could do some of the guiding. I would take one of the small boats and a couple of the party. At that time we did a lot of rowing while the party was casting, and caught a lot of fish. Sometimes we would go two weeks and never see another boat. I enjoyed this. We would shoot alligators, birds, and catch fish. We had a married couple as cook and steward, Carrie and Miller. Carrie could cook anything and make it taste good. Elmo Pearce was the engineer and chief guide. He taught me how to run the 28 foot cruiser we towed along.

The *Nepenthe* had two big ice boxes that carried about a thousand pounds of block ice each. The top deck was like a canopy. When it rained the canopy caught fresh water, and it was piped right into the fresh water tank, and that was our fresh water supply. She carried a lot of gasoline, enough to run the 28 foot cruiser also.

We had another 18 foot skiff that had an inboard engine in it, and Elmo would usually take that one. Captain Fred would take the 28 foot cruiser and the rowing skiff, and I usually went with him. When we got to where we were going to fish he would cut me loose in the skiff, with one or two of the party.

This one party we chartered, I never will forget. It was Mr. D. A. Dalton, owner of a steel mill up in Ohio. He had four buddies with him and they all brought their shot guns and fly rods. On this trip, Captain Fred had hired his brother, Perry Roberts who owned a 30 foot cruiser, to go along with us. At the last minute, Captain Perry was sick and could not go.

Captain Fred asked John Mickle if he would take over. John was just out of the Navy from World War II, and was glad to get the job. The Mickles were a great family. John had an older brother, Mack Mickle, who was a famous tarpon guide in Boca Grande. He had a younger brother, Ward Mickle who later on ran a boat for the Marine Patrol. They also had two sisters, Margaret, a reporter for the News Press, and Lucy, a housewife.

John Mickle was a short man about 5' 6" and weighed about 250 pounds. He was a real comical man and told of these stories about his life. I don't know if they were all true or not, but they were so funny you really enjoyed hearing them. So every evening when we finished fishing and eating, John would tell his stories. The *Nepenthe's* deck house was screened in, and they would go up there, drink, and play cards until about midnight.

One story John told when he was at Boca Grande was about him and his partner trout fishing. At that time, the railroad from Boca Grande ran up through Arcadia, and on up through the phosphate mines. John and his partner both had boats and girlfriends in Arcadia. So every Friday night they would catch the train to see the girls. To get to the train station they had to go under the railroad bridge. The bridge tender had a little dock built down under the bridge where he would go at night and catch shrimp with a dip net. One Friday night John and his partner were going to catch the train. They took both boats in case one had to leave before the other. John was following his partner under the bridge because there were only a few spans you could cross under. He went under the bridge and heard his partner hit something. He didn't think much about it at the time, so they went on, caught the train and spent the weekend in Arcadia. They returned Sunday evening and got off the train, and went to a little beer joint at the foot of the bridge, where they tied up their boats.

The bridge tender was there, and he looked like he had been in a fight, or an accident, with cuts and bruises all over his head. They asked him what happened. He said he was down under the bridge Friday night, catching shrimp, when two boats came along. The first boat hit his dock and knocked it down, and he went over board, the next boat came along and ran over him. John said this was their last trip to Arcadia.

Mr. Dalton got to where he wanted to cut cards with me for money. I didn't have much money then, only made 100 dollars a month. Mr. Dalton would cut for like 5 dollars a card for high card, and I got into him for 40 dollars. That was a lot of money for me. One night we finished playing cards and went out on the bow of the boat. She had this strong back to hold the cross beams up. I would jump and catch the beam and do chin ups, and touch my toes up on the ceiling. Mr. Dalton was there watching me do that. John Mickle said, "I bet Mr. Dalton can't do that."

Mr. Dalton answered back; "I'll bet you double or nothing I can do that for what you owe me."

"That's a bet," I said.

Mr. Dalton was another one of these heavy short men. He was bigger than John Mickle, and was probably about 5' 7" and weighed about 250 or 300 pounds. He jumped up there. He strained, and I thought the whole top of the cabin was coming down. He could not make it, barely getting his feet off the ground. So I got my 40 dollars back. I didn't owe him, and I was really relieved!

We would go into the rivers and the party would sit out on the bow of the boat with their shotguns, and any bird that flew up they would try to shoot it.

Coming back, they decided we were going into Everglades City. It had been a long charter, it seemed like a month. We had been up to the head of Shark River and hadn't seen a boat. On the way back, John and I took the cruiser he was running, and went into Broad Creek, north of Shark River. I had never seen so many tarpon! They were fly-casting, you could get one almost every time, and the tarpon would jump out of the water. Mr. Dalton decided he would let someone else cast, so that when the tarpon would jump, he could try to shoot him with his shotgun. I don't think he ever hit one, but they sure had a great time.

We went on into Everglades City and Captain Fred had his wife come down to pick him up, to spend a night or two with her. He left John Mickle, Elmo Pearce, the Millers, and Mr. Dalton's party on the *Nepenthe*.

Sometime during the night the tide got real high, and the *Nepenthe* hung up by the guardrail, over the pilings. She was listed over on her side; it looked as if she was about to turn over. I was sleeping in the engine room and was awakened by dishes falling off the shelves. When I ran out on deck to see what was happening, the tide had fallen, but one side of the boat was still up on the dock. I was not sure what to do. I took the cruiser and tied a line onto the *Nepenthe*, got off broad side, then snatched her off the pilings. When she came down off the pilings she was really rolling and pitching. Old man Dalton came running out of the cabin scared to death. He was hung over from the night before, and I thought he was going to have a fit. When I told him what had happened he said, "Well, that's all right." Captain Fred came back that day. We packed up and got out of there, and made it back to Fort Myers that afternoon.

The next day with the same party, we went up to Boca Grande to do some tarpon fishing. We anchored the *Nepenthe* just north of Useppa Island.

Fishing Boca Grande takes a lot of local knowledge and John Mickle had that. Mr. Dalton latched onto John and he wanted me to go along. We took the cruiser that John was running, the *Yogi*. Every morning when Mr. Dalton got up, he would start drinking. We would load up on the *Yogi* and take off for the pass. Captain Fred would take the other cruiser, *Who Cares* and take the rest of the party to the pass.

To fish Boca Grande Pass, you drift with the tide. By the time we arrived there Mr. Dalton would be pretty drunk. He would tell John he was going down in the cabin and take a nap, and for us to take turns fishing. While one of us ran the boat, the other one would fish, so it would look like Mr. Dalton was fishing. Every day we caught tarpon, some of them were in the 90 pound class to 100 pound class. We released most of them, but when we would catch a real big one, Mr. Dalton would make us take him back to the Nepenthe, string him up so the rest of the party could see him, and he could brag about catching tarpon. Needless to say, Captain Fred wasn't happy over this situation.

We finally finished up Boca Grande fishing and went back to Fort Myers. When Mr. Dalton was ready to leave, he gave Captain Fred $100, and gave the cook and the rest of us $40 apiece, which was more tip money that I had ever seen, for just doing my job. That was the last charter we had for that year.

One of the other owners of the *Nepenthe* came down later that summer. The boat actually belonged to 3 people. The head man was Mr. Hannah that owned the Cleveland News in Cleveland, Ohio. There were two other partners, I don't remember their names. But anyway, one of them got in an argument with Captain Fred. He tried to get Captain Fred to drink with him, but Captain Fred was an alcoholic and couldn't drink, and knew the results if he did. Captain Fred got real smart with him and they almost came to blows. That owner went back home and wrote back a letter to Captain Fred, terminating him. They told him they didn't need him on the boat anymore. So I said I was finished. The boat went into storage.

Then I went back to work at the Daniels boat yard, and John Mickle had been appointed dock master at the Fort Myers Yacht Basin. He really made a good place out of the Yacht Basin, for transit boats and local boat owners.

John had a little office about 10x10. A cousin of mine, Bud Daniels worked at the boat yard with me. He decided to play a trick on John. He had caught an armadillo and decided on just the place for it. Bud jimmied open one of the windows in John's office and dropped the armadillo inside, just to be a surprise.

About two days later an article came out in the Fort Myers News Press, "Dock Master finds armadillo in office." The article went on to explain how people out in Texas have armadillos for pets, and evidently one of his customers, or boat owner, had left one in his office. Bud and I got a kick out of this!

Within four or five months they had hired a new Captain on the *Nepenthe*, Captain Hugh Goldie. He was an old timer and a really good man. He contacted me and said the owners wanted to know if I would go back to work for them. They had also let go Elmo Pearce, and asked me if I could run the engines. I told them I could. I had watched Elmo and he had let me run the engines a time or two, so I didn't think I would have any problems. I hired back on for a second year.

The *Nepenthe* was built in 1909 on the north side of the river, across from Fort Myers. Captain Eddie Johnson was her first owner as far back as I can remember. When the war came along there wasn't much charter business so Captain Eddie sold her to Mr. Hannah. Captain Eddie was an old timer from Marco Island. He was a Swede, his people coming over from Sweden.

They had to have an engineer on the *Nepenthe* because she didn't have remote controls to the pilot house. She had signals which were controlled by cables from the pilot house to the engine room. One bell meant slow ahead, and then there was a jingle that meant speed up to cruising speed. Two bells meant to reverse. If you were running at cruising speed, and got one bell, that meant slow down, and another bell, meant go into neutral. If you were running cruising speed, and got four bells, it meant slow down and go into reverse. She had two engines so that meant she had two sets of bells. One had a soft tone the other had a sharp ring, so you could tell the difference.

When Captain Goldie took over, we took her out to Hansen's

Boatyard, up on Orange River, about five miles east of Fort Myers. We hauled out the *Nepenthe* to do some caulking on her and painted her inside and out.

Captain Goldie's daughter was married to Albert Hansen. He was one of the owners of the boatyard, along with his dad, and brother Siegfried. They were Danes that came over from Denmark. That was a big place, with big storage buildings. They also had an engine repair shop.

The Hansens were fine people, dedicated and compassionate. Albert had three sons, Edward, Ernest, and Tommy, and one daughter Christen.

Albert lived on the property with his family. They had a Model A Ford. Edward hadn't got his license yet, so he let me have the car to take the kids for rides.

Christen was a pretty girl, and I think she was my first love. I don't think she ever knew it, but I did. Nothing ever happened between us.

When the *Nepenthe* was ready, we finished the season. Then I just hung around the Yacht Basin for a while.

CHAPTER FIVE

Captain Paul Wright from Bayou La Batre, Alabama, purchased an 83 foot air sea rescue boat in Charleston, South Carolina, and brought it to Fort Myers. While he was there he sold it to a Frenchman, Mr. Roe Dupree, with an agreement to deliver it to Lafayette, La.

Captain Paul asked John Mickle, who was then dock master, if he knew anyone that could go along as engineer. John told him about me. So Captain Paul asked me if I could run those engines. I told him if their name was engine, I could run them. They were 500 horse power Hall Scot gasoline engines. He asked me if I could go to Lafayette with him. I said, "I don't have anything else to do."

He said, "Get your clothes; we will pull out at daylight tomorrow."

We ran down to Sanibel Island and set a course for the mouth of the Mississippi River, straight across. We had 2,500 gallons of gasoline. The plan was just running one engine at a time, and running fairly slow to conserve fuel. Captain Paul decided to run both engines, about 1,000 rpm. He figured she was doing about 10 knots, and we ran all that night, all the next day, and the next night. At 2:00 AM, we were supposed to pick up the lights off the Mississippi River.

It's a funny thing. If you have ever made a trip like this, and you know you are supposed to see lights, you will see them. I don't know whether it's an optical illusion, or what. Anyway, everybody on board thought they saw them.

We stayed right on compass course, ran till daylight, and running short of fuel. We didn't have any navigational equipment except a compass, and our running time, and not sure of our speed. Evidently, she wasn't running as fast as Captain Paul had figured.

We saw a ship coming. Captain Paul didn't know whether she was coming out of Mobile or New Orleans, but he turned around and tried to catch her to get a location from them. She was one of those victory ships and was really making some time. We couldn't even keep up with her. We blinked them on the search light, but they didn't answer or slow down, so we turned around and headed due north.

Captain Paul said we better make land fall as soon as possible, probably into Mississippi or Alabama. We ran till about noon, then, sighted the light house at the entrance to Mobile Bay. We entered the Intracostal Waterway there, and went on into Bayou La Batre. We had about 100 gallons of fuel left, so we fueled up there, and spent the night.

The next day, we started up the Mississippi sound, towards New Orleans, and about noon, I started smelling gas real strong in the engine room. I went down and saw one of the fuel pumps spraying gasoline around a bolt. I took a wrench and tried to tighten it, and it broke off. Then I had a steady stream of gasoline spraying all over the engine room. I ran up and told Captain Paul what had happened.

Those motors, if you didn't idle them down for four or five minutes before you shut them down, would backfire through the carburetor. I didn't know if we had that much time or not. I had already witnessed a boat catch on fire at the boat yard. He knew, and I knew, but nobody else on board knew, what was happening. I said, "What are we going to do, Captain?"

He said, "Close all the fuel valves, and close up the engine room so she can't get any air, and come up on deck."

So I did. She kept on slowing down until she ran out of fuel, and didn't backfire the first time. I didn't know about anybody else, but I was praying. I went to Captain Paul and told him, "The Lord sure was with us this time."

Captain Paul answered back "He sure was!"

Captain Paul was a Mason, so I knew he believed in God. He told Mr. Dupree and the rest of the crew this was a good fishing spot, and we had just stopped to do some fishing, No one else had a clue about the engine room problem.

I disconnected that fuel pump and bypassed it. She had three fuel pumps on each engine. We got her aired out and got under way, again headed for New Orleans. We went through the Rigules and into the Mississippi River, and up to the Intracoastal Canal, headed for Morgan City, Louisiana. When we arrived, there was a lot of activity, and a lot of big oil boats. We stayed the night.

That boat had engine room annunciators, and was engine room controlled, using dials with levers. When the Captain wanted slow speed, he pushed his control in the pilot house, and it indicated in the engine room to the engineer, and he answered back. As we started to back out of the slip, Captain Paul would ring me for reverse. I put her in slow reverse, which was 250 rpm. All of a sudden, I heard bells ringing, and the annunciator handles were going back and forth, and I didn't know what to do. She had this little escape hatch that opened up into the pilot house, and all of a sudden I heard it open, Captain Paul shouted down "The tide has got me! Give her hell!"

I knew what he needed then, so I gave him full reverse. We got out of there, every thing settled down, and we went on to Lafayette, Louisiana.

Roe Dupree was in the oil business and that was when they first started the off shore oil exploration. He took a liking to me for some reason and said, "Why don't you stay on here? I will send you to school to learn geodetic surveying. There is a big future in this." This is a deal where the boat runs along and drops dynamite charges, and when the charges go off they take these seismographic soundings to see if oil is there. It first sounded like a good deal to me, so I stayed on.

Mr. Dupree had a ship yard in Lafayette where we had the boat tied up. I decided quickly that I didn't like that part of the country. So I told Mr. Dupree, I thought I would go back home. This was a good opportunity, but it just wasn't my bag.

Captain Paul had told me before he left, if I decided to go back to Fort Myers, to stop at Bayou La Batre and see him. I caught the bus back to Bayou La Batre and Captain Paul was there. That was right after the war.

You could make bids on boats, and Captain Paul had just bought a 40 foot motor launch that was in Meshu, Louisiana. It was in an old government base that had to dispose of boats.

He wasn't married at that time and had a little cottage down on the Mississippi sound, and he said, "Why don't you stay here for a while?" We will go get that 40 footer and convert her to a shrimp boat, and try some shrimping."

That sounded like a real adventure to me, so I told him I would stay. I really liked this part of the country, and thought I would like to go shrimping and oystering. I had saved up about $700 or $800, so I didn't have to worry about money for a while.

Captain Paul's old friend, Fred Johnson had four boys and one girl. I think Tom was the oldest. And there was another one I never met. Billy was about my age, and the girl, Ollie, was about 14, and another younger boy called Boots.

Captain Fred took us over to Meshu in his little 35 foot shrimper. Captain Paul told Fred we had to do some repair work on the 40 footer, caulking and maybe a plank or two. This little shrimper had a 35 hp caterpillar tractor engine in her. We all loaded up, Captain Paul, Captain Fred, his two youngest boys, and I to go over there and started repairing the 40 footer. We were camping on the shrimp boat, or sometime on the barge that the 40 footer was on, or wherever we could find a place to sleep.

The mosquitoes were really bad. We built a smudge fire to smoke them off. There was a bridge across the Intracoastal Waterway. One night the bridge tender came down and said, "Boys you all are going to have to put out these fires. I can't even see the cars coming down the road, and I can't tell when it is safe to open the draw bridge when a boat comes along." So we had to put our smudge fires out and pull our blankets up over our heads. We spent another night or two there, and finally got the boat ready to launch. We put her overboard and she didn't leak a drop. We started towing her back to Bayou La Batre, Alabama.

The little shrimper we were on had a long propeller shaft and an intermediate bearing. It had fuel drums for fuel tanks, and one of her fuel tanks sprung a leak, and the fuel that had accumulated in the bilge had eaten the bearing out, and she was really rattling. We shut her down and took a pair of leather shoes, and made a leather bearing. We pumped all of the tractor fuel out of the bilge, and started on down the Mississippi sound.

I was riding on the 40 footer (the boat we had in tow), keeping a check on her. About noon that day we hit a bad squall. We had to slow down, but we charged on along and made it back to Bayou La Batre the next day.

We went to work on the 40 footer, decked her over, and built a wheel house on her. She had a Buda diesel in her and we got it running. We loaded a shrimp net with about a 50 foot trawl. You had to pick it up by hand, as we didn't have a power winch. We would shrimp all day and anchor up at night. The company had run boats that would come along side while you were shrimping, take your shrimp and give you a ticket for them. When you came in, you could go to the fish house and settle up. I shrimped for a couple months and then the season ended.

Captain Paul and I had a little disagreement. He loaned me one of his cars one night and I tore the muffler off it. I just happened to make the mistake of running over some tree stumps! He kind of got mad about that, and I kind of flew off the handle too.

Captain Fred wanted me to go oystering for him. Oyster season had just started. I told him I would, so he said, "Why don't you come, move in with me and the family?"

I moved in with them, and built a 20 foot oyster skiff. I put a Chevrolet car motor in it and started out oystering. That was really rough work. First, you tong them up, load them on deck, then cull them out, and throw all the good ones in the hole of the boat. You keep doing this until you have all you can haul, or all you are able to pick up. As you arrive at the dock, you start to open them, or pay some one else to do it for you. But anyway, I enjoyed it. I was my own boss and I liked that.

As I came in one night, there was a telegram waiting for me. It said, if I wanted to see my granddad alive, I better come home. They had put him in the hospital with pneumonia and they didn't think he would live much longer. He was pretty old, so I figured they were right. I decided to catch the bus to Fort Myers. Soon after that my granddad got all right.

I wrote Captain Fred to give my boat to Billy, his son who was about my age. They really needed it, being rather poor, and trying to survive like everyone else at that time.

CHAPTER SIX

This friend of mine, Bill Kepler, had told me earlier that he was going over to the east coast and try to get a yacht job. He told me if I ever heard from him, I had better come. Soon after leaving, he wrote back saying, I have a good job for you, with good pay. If you are ready to go to sea, come over to Daytona Beach.

I went over there to meet with Bill. He had a job on a beautiful little 35 foot sail boat, *Gaviota*, belonging to Houland Spencer of the Bahamas. We really fixed her up, from stem to stern.

Mr. Spencer had a lady friend down in Palm Beach, Mrs. T. W. Griggs, who owned a 57 foot Yacht, *Berania*. It was at the Daytona Beach Boat Works being overhauled. Mrs. Griggs was trying to hire Bill away from Mr. Spencer to run her boat.

Bill told me we have to take both yachts down to Palm Beach, where Mrs. Griggs lived. First, he and I took the *Gaviota*, tied her up there, and I stayed on board. Bill and Mr. Spencer's cook, Quinton, an English boy, went back to Daytona Beach to get the *Berania*. They had to hurry back with her to Palm Beach, to make her ready for the Bahamas.

Berania was registered in the Bahamas, she was only allowed so much time in the United States, then go back to Nassau.

I had always wanted to go to the Bahamas, and when Bill said, "I had better take Johnny with me," I was ready!

Quinton had already had to leave because he was a British subject, and his visa had expired. He went to Harbor Island.

In the meantime, Mr. Spencer had agreed to let Bill go to work for Mrs. Griggs.

We loaded up the *Berania*, and Mrs. Griggs, Mr. Spencer, Bill and I ran down to Miami. That was the jumping off place for Nassau, so we refueled and spent the night. The next morning it was blowing about 25 knots out of the east. Bill told Mr. Spencer it was going to be real rough. Mr. Spencer said no, it would be all right. Bill said, "Well, all right, it's your boat." So we started out through Government Cut, the main inlet in Miami. The first sea broke over the bow and right on back over the wheel house, and filled up the aft cockpit. Mr. Spencer hollered at Bill to turn around and go back. Bill said, we can't turn around in this chop, she'll roll over. We will have to go on out into the ocean where the seas aren't so steep.

In that cut, when the tide is running out against a strong east wind, it makes a real bad sea condition. Bill was a good sailor and he knew what he was talking about. We eased on out past the sea buoy where the seas were a little father apart, turned around, and started back through the cut. About half way in, a big sea caught her under the stern, one motor quit, and she was headed for the rock jetty at about 20 knots. Bill finally got the other engine started and brought her back around. I really thought it was the end of the line that day. I was glad to get tied up to the dock again. We decided to wait over night and see what the weather was going to do. It calmed down.   The next day was real pretty, so we headed on over to Cat Key, arriving about noon to spend the night. The next day, we headed on across the Bahama Banks towards N. W. Channel light. We ran about 5 or 6 hours, and as Bill was looking, he spotted a light.

He said, "That is not the N. W. Channel Light. That's Great Stirrup Key light." The compass was way off.

We didn't know it, but when you ran the generator, it set up a magnetic field and pulled the compass off about 20 degrees. We went on in to Great Stirrup and anchored up. It started blowing that night.

There is a channel you can go down through the banks to Chub Key, which is a jumping off place to Nassau. Bill said he didn't know it well enough to try it. This old man and a young boy, both native Bahamians, came out in a little sailing dinghy to try to sell us some fish. We bought some from him. He said he knew the way down through the channel, and if it was still blowing tomorrow, and if we would tow his dinghy, so he would have a way back, he would guide us.

Bill was a little skeptical about the whole deal but he decided to go along with it. The next morning it was still blowing, so the old man and the boy came out to the boat. We decided to leave anyway. We were about half way there, his dinghy kept getting lower in the water, and I saw she was taking on a lot of spray. I told Bill she was sinking. Bill said she would be all right and the old man agreed with him. About an hour later I went back to check on her, and she was down. I told Bill we better stop. We stopped, and the dinghy went right on down to the bottom. He had a bunch of rocks in the bilge for ballast and it was just enough to sink her. The old man was really upset. He didn't know what to do; I thought he was going to cry. I was young then and a pretty good diver. It was only 8 or 10 feet deep, so I put on my swim suit and went over board, and threw the rocks out of her. She came to the surface, and I bailed her out for him. Mrs. Griggs really got off on that. She thought I was a big savior or something. She was a real compassionate person and felt sorry for the old man and boy. She wanted to hire me to stay right on her boat all the time.

We went on to Whale Key, an island that Betty Carstairs owned. She was a famous British Lady. It was one of the islands just north of Chub Key. It was still blowing so we anchored up in the harbor, and sent the old man back. She paid him, and gave him some potatoes, and some canned goods, so he would have something to eat on the way back. He was real happy over this. We stayed there a couple days. It finally calmed down and we went on across to Nassau, and tied up at Yacht Haven.

Mr. Spenser wanted me to go back and get on the *Gaviota*, as there wasn't anybody there to care for it. Mrs. Griggs and I flew back to Miami, and had her limousine come and pick us up at the airport. We stayed there about a month, and went sailing one time.

Mr. Spenser decided to take the *Gaviota* over to Harbor Island. He contacted Basil Symonette, a Bahamian that knew the waters over there, and had worked for him before. So Mr. Spencer said we will get Basil and you, and take the *Gaviota* over to Harbor Island. Basil's father was Roland Symonette, the governor of the Bahamas. I didn't know that until years later.

In the meantime Mr. Spencer had bought another boat, a 30 foot Jersey sea skiff. We got this other boy, Bigley, a friend of Basils, to run the sea skiff. We took the two boats down to Miami and hung around down there two or three days, waiting for it to calm down. It was in the spring time and it usually blows every day. We finally caught a fairly calm day and started out, and went down and out around Cape Florida. Basil said the father south we started out, the better of we would be. We could take advantage of the Gulf Stream that flows north. The wind was out of the southeast at about 15 knots, and about half way to Bimini, it started blowing. We shortened sail, and took the mainsail down. She was a ketch rig, so that left the jib and mizzen up, which was all the sail she needed. About dark, we sighted North Bimini. It was southeast so that made it a beat straight into the wind. We started tacking into the wind and it really got rough. The wind got up to about 25 or 30 knots. She would take a sea over the bow, then roll down and put her rail under. We just weren't making any headway at all, so Basil said, let's start the engine, take the rest of the sails down, and drive her straight into it.

Then she really took a beating for about three or four hours. She was a strong little boat and I wasn't worried about it.

We finally got to where we were ready to cross the bar, and all of these little dinghies with some local boys who wanted to pilot us in. Basil knew the channel. He told them we didn't need them. We went on into Bimini and spent the night there, and I think we spent the next night. Then, as we started across the Bahama Banks toward N. W. Light, I remembered the trip before, when we couldn't find the N. W. Light, and wound up at great Stirrup Key. I asked Basil if he thought we should go that way. He said, "Yes. No problem." We sailed all that day and into the night, with the wind dead ahead, tacking all the way. Sometime, early in the morning, before daylight, I was down below sleeping, and Basil called me out.

He said, "I want you to see N. W. Channel Light in case you never see it again." We had hit it right on the head.

I said, "Oh, it looks like you have done a good job getting us here." We went on into the tongue of the ocean and headed for Nassau. The next day the wind died off to a flat calm, so we started up the engine, and ran for a couple of hours, then ran out of gasoline. We hadn't fueled up in Bimini. We hoisted sail again. By then the wind had picked up a little bit, and we got into Nassau about midnight. We anchored up right off Yacht Haven, owned by Bobby Symonett, Basil's brother. They were just building it then. The sea skiff, in the meantime, had already come across and was waiting in Nassau for us. The next day we bought groceries, fueled up, and headed for Spanish Wells. We had a fair wind and made it into Spanish Wells that night, tying up at a dock in the harbor. Basil had two or three buddies that came down and played cards till about midnight. The next day we headed around to Harbor Island. That's the worst passage in the Bahamas, Spanish Wells to Harbor Island. Basil said he knew it, so I wasn't worried. There wasn't much wind so we motored on around.

We got in about 3 o'clock that afternoon and went on down to Mr. Spencer's, a big house on the south end of the island. It was a beautiful place, right in the center of the island. You could look to the east and see the ocean, and to the west and see the harbor; it was on a high hill. The island is only about a mile wide there. Basil stayed on about two weeks and we went over all the varnish on the *Gaviota*.

Then Basil said he was going back to Miami. He had another boat there, and had a little sailing school. He wanted me to go back with him, but I told him I was going to stay on in the Bahamas. I liked it there. I had always wanted to go to the Bahamas anyway. So Basil, and Bigley, the boy that brought the sea skiff over, went back to Miami. That left me in charge of the sailboat, the sea skiff, as well as two Bahama sailing dinghies.

We went into town twice a week, to pick up supplies. I would take the sea skiff to go to the store. That's where I met my first wife, Elsie Albury. I started courting her, and usually went downtown every night in one of the dinghies to see her. I usually got back home around 10 or 11 o'clock. This went on for two or three months.

One night, when I was returning back to the boat house that I usually stayed in, by the waters edge, Mr. Spencer called out to me to come up to the house. He was alone so he wanted me to stay up there with him that night. On this one particular night, one of the colored boys, Tom Sawyer came in and woke us up, trying to find me.

Mr. Spencer said, "Yes, he is down in the other bedroom,"

Tom said, "Well, the sailing dinghy is gone."

He said two prisoners had escaped out of Nassau prison, and had gone over to Eleuthra, the big island right across from Harbor Island. There were many families who had farms over there, and the prisoners had murdered one of them. They took his dinghy and came over to Harbor Island, broke into the store where we bought supplies, and they had disappeared from there. He had just come back to the house, and the dinghy was gone. He knew I always used that one because it was a pretty little Abaco-built dinghy, and it sailed really well.

Mr. Spencer said, "Better go try to find that dinghy." He gave us an old 30-30 rifle to take along.

We went down, got the sea skiff and took off up town, to get permission from the commissioner of the island to see if we could go try to capture them, and get our boat back. The commissioner of the island was Raymond Higgs. He was engaged to Elsie's older sister, Ruth. He told us yes, go ahead.

By this time we had gathered up eight or ten local boys to go with us. We went down to the city dock where we had left the sea skiff. It was a full moon. I don't know why, but I just headed straight across the harbor. We ran just a few minutes and sighted the sail of the dinghy.

I said, "Well, there she is."

We ran up on them. My sea skiff had a forward cockpit that a couple of people could ride up on the bow, and a couple of the fellows were up there. They were Buster and Tom Sawyer. I said, "I am going to run up on them, and one of you jump down in there, while the other one holds the rifle on them, and we will try to capture them."

We had a surprise when we got to the dinghy; there was no one in it. They saw us coming, lashed down the sheet and tiller, then jumped overboard, and the dinghy kept on sailing. We took down the sail and took her in tow. I knew the direction they came from, so I headed back that way, and we came up on them swimming. One of our crew tried to shoot, but the old rifle wouldn't fire, so they hit him over the head, and he went down. The other one was a real good swimmer. I would run the boat up so we could reach him, and he would dive under the boat, and come up on the other side. So I told Buster that they would have to get in the dinghy and paddle up to him, because I just couldn't maneuver fast enough. They were really afraid of him. They thought he had a gun or something. I told them he didn't have a gun, but even if he did, it would be wet and wouldn't shoot. I finally talked them into getting in the dinghy. They went out, captured him, brought him back, and threw him over in the cockpit of the sea skiff. He was buck naked, scared to death, and pooped all over the deck! We tried to find the other one, but I guess he drowned. The one we captured said, "The other one wasn't much of a swimmer."

When we arrived back, there were about a hundred people standing on the dock. They wanted to hang him without a trial. I finally talked them out of it. The commissioner took him and locked him up. He told us that the officials from Nassau would be down.

They came down the next day in a sea plane, and flew out over the area where we captured the one prisoner. All they saw was a couple of big sharks. They never found the other one, so we figured those sharks had eaten him. That kind of made a hero out of me, going out and catching the murderers. They took him back to Nassau, tried him, and hung him. I stayed on in Harbor Island a couple of months after that.

This is a song the Bahama boys made up about me, after we captured the prisoners. Tom Sawyer, Buster and Joe thought I was just the greatest!

> His name is Morgan
> But it ain't J.P.
> He don't own no R.R. Company.
>
> He ain't rich
> And not too smart
> But wins the best
> Of all our hearts!
>
> He is not so big

But he is strong,
Just keeps on working
All day long.

Fishing and sailing
Is his plan
He is our Captain.
He's our man!

I just turned 18 years old, and I thought I had to register for the draft. I told Mr. Spencer I would have to take a leave of absence, or quit, because I had to go back to the U S and register. I heard that the Korean War had just begun. I had been away from home a long time, and was kind of home sick anyway. I told Elsie I was leaving, and wasn't sure I would be back.

I flew back home, and went up to the draft board, and told them I had been over in the Bahamas, and came back to register for the draft. He told me this wasn't necessary, if I wanted to stay over there, I wouldn't have to register. I told him I wasn't a draft dodger, and wanted to register anyway.

In the meantime, my mother and sister Shirley had moved back to Fort Myers, into our old house that my dad had bought before he died. They had been living in Gainesville, Florida with my stepfather, an instructor there at the university. I really didn't know what I wanted to do.

Elsie wrote a letter saying she really wanted me to come back over there. She had talked to Mr. Spencer and he said I could have my job back. I liked it there, so I decided to fly back and see what was going on.

Elsie, her younger sister Francis, their mother and her mother, who was still alive, all asked me if I didn't want to stay there. Both of the older sisters were married and gone. They had an extra bedroom.

I asked Mr. Spencer if it was all right if I stayed in town at night. He said no problem. He had a Bahama couple that cooked for him, and stayed out there all the time. I started living downtown, and every morning, I'd walk to work. It was only about a mile. I would spend the day with Mr. Spencer working on the boats, and messing around. We would go sailing once in a while, and did a lot of lobstering and gathering conch.

Elsie's oldest sister, Percis, was married to Carlyle Albury. His father was an airline agent for Bahama Airways at that time. They owned two stores on Harbor Island.

Elsie had a cousin named Kenneth Johnson. He was building a 26 foot charter boat and I spent a lot of time with him talking about fishing and boating. He was a good sailor and fisherman. The tourist trade had just started after the war was over, and there was a lot of charter fishing business.

I stayed in Harbor Island another four or five months. Elsie and I finally decided to get married. She wanted to leave right away and come over here, to Miami or Fort Myers. I didn't really want to leave because I had a good job and liked it over there. I was planning on starting a little freight business with the sea skiff we had. Mr. Spencer had agreed to let me use it. I was going to run to Hatchet Bay, which was only about 20 miles south on Eleuthra. There was a big farm down there that raised cattle and chickens. That was where all the milk, eggs and meat came from, for Harbor Island. It went from Hatchet Bay to Nassau, which was about a 70 mile run each way. To go direct from Hatchet Bay to Harbor Island you can save a lot of time and money. It looked like a real good deal to me, but Elsie wanted to leave. I agreed to do what she wanted to do. We had a real big church wedding. A couple days later we flew to Miami, and had to stay there for a week while she got her papers straightened out. Then we went on to Fort Myers, and moved into the house with my mother and sister.

CHAPTER SEVEN

It wasn't too long after Elsie and I came home, my granddad Jack Collier passed away. He was 81 years old. He had pneumonia, and I guess he was just old and tired.

I went back to work at the boatyard. My uncle Bruce Collier had gotten out of the Navy and was working at the boatyard too. I was very close to him. He was my mother's only brother. Along about that time he started doing a lot of hunting. He had a Model A Ford cut down, kind of a swamp buggy rig. He and Lois, and another couple were going on this hunting trip. He got down to Estero, and was going around a curve, and lost control of his truck. It flipped over, pinned him under it, the gasoline poured down on him, the truck caught on fire and set him on fire. He finally got out from under it and started running. They caught him, threw some blankets over him, put out the fire, and took him back to Fort Myers to the hospital. His wife called and told me he was critically burned over 70% of his body. She said that he wasn't going to make it. I went to the hospital to be with him his last few hours.

This was all confusing to me, and it seemed strange that all of this could happen like it did. He had been in the Navy and went through the invasion of Okinawa, Iwo Jima, the Philippines, and on to Japan, and came back and got killed in a car wreck. I guess it was one of those things, you don't know when it's your time to go.

Bruce was really an artist. He could start a boat and build it from stem to stern, and when he finished building it, put a gold leaf name on the transom, and letters or name, on the bow. He had painted several pictures, and was a sign painter on the side, while he was building boats. He left behind his wife Lois and two sons, Robert Bruce and Tommy.

Lois bought a 12 foot skiff for Robert Bruce, and I had a 10 hp. Mercury Outboard engine we put on it. He and I went fishing and claming a lot together.

During this time I was still working at Daniels Bros. boatyard, but was getting very restless.

Along came my friend Bill Kepler, on his way to New York, with the yacht *Berania*. Mrs. Griggs told Bill to try to find and hire me back again. I was more than ready because the sea was calling me back again.

I told Bill I would go up to New York with him and help out for a while. We met over in Palm Beach about a week later. I had to give Uncle Frank and Henry some notice that I was leaving. Bill's wife was a Hisler. Her name was Arzelia; they called her Zeke. She was from Rainey Slough, a little place just north of LaBelle, Florida. I don't think there is anything there but a bridge now. She liked to brag about being from Rainy Slough. People thought this was real funny. She made the trip up to New York with us.

We were about a month getting there, and after we arrived, we went into 79th Street Yacht Basin. That was on the Hudson River. We did quite a bit of cruising up the Hudson River and Long Island Sound. We made a trip to Connecticut with Mrs. Griggs daughter and her husband. As we anchored up in this harbor, I think it was Greenwich, Connecticut, a bunch of drunks circled around us in a boat, whooping and hollering. All of a sudden they lost control of the boat and rammed us, broad side, and knocked a hole in the *Berania* about six feet long. We had to go into a ship yard on Long Island for repairs.

After we went into the shipyard, Bill asked me if I could handle everything. He had his sailboat down in Annapolis, Maryland and wanted to leave. There wasn't much to do, just wait until they finished the work.

In about two weeks Elsie called me. She had moved down to Miami with my mother and sister. My stepfather had gotten a job down there at the University of Miami as an instructor. They needed me back home. She was pregnant with my oldest son Paul. I called Bill and told him I was going to have to leave him. He came up and took charge of the *Berania* and I caught the train back to Miami.

When I arrived I didn't know what I was going to do. I walked down around the Yacht basin on the Miami River.

Basil Symonette had bought a 50 foot schooner, to charter, but it needed quite a bit of work. I helped him fix up the decks and the rest of the repair. He had been down to the Virgin Islands, and had a charter business going. He wanted me to go back to the Virgin Islands with him, but I didn't want to do that, as I had been gone away from home long enough. With a new family coming along I didn't feel right about it.

When I called Uncle Frank in Fort Myers, I asked him if he had any work for me. He said yes, come on up and we will build some more boats. So I moved back home.

Along that time my first son was born. I asked Elsie what she wanted to name him, and she wanted to call him Paul, after Paul in the Bible. I said that would be fine. His second name would be Henry, after my Uncle Henry that I thought so much of. He had helped me learn, to build boats, and to be a good Christian person.

We built a few boats and I got into outboard racing. I built an 11-foot class "A" race boat, and finally had it running pretty good so that I could win a few races.

I met a man named June Wheeler. He had a factory built race boat. He liked to run it, but didn't want to race, very much. He decided to finance me, and took me all over the state racing. I remember this one race in Sarasota. As I went around the first turn, it was pretty rough and I flipped over, but it threw me clear of the boat. The boat behind me ran over my boat, his propeller cut right through the side of it. When my head came up out of the water, the first thing that I heard was an outboard roaring in my ear. I don't know how he missed me. I guess the Lord was with me. Another boat came out and towed me in to the dock.

We went back to Fort Myers for repairs. I finally got it to running 46 mph, 2 miles over the world's record at that time. I didn't have much trouble winning races after that.

I worked on for a couple of years for Daniels Brothers and in the meantime a cousin of mine, Guye Daniels (he was Uncle Henry's son) had moved down to Naples, and was foreman at Gulf Coast Marine. He had offered me a job there, making about twice as much money as I was at Daniels Brothers. I talked it over with Uncle Frank and it didn't seem like he could raise my pay, so I decided to go down and work for Gulf Coast Marine.

Jim Dunn was president there at that time, and I first worked under him for a while. We built a 26 foot cabin boat, an 18 foot open boat, for some local people.

After I was at Gulf Coast Marine for a while, Guye decided he wanted to go in business for himself. Henry Espenlaub owned all of that property, so they divided it up. Guye took the north end, and Gulf Coast Marine kept the south end.

Henry's brother-in-law was Eddie Frank, president of the Bank of Naples. Eddie was credited with building the first swamp buggy. Henry was quite the character. He had a jeep he named, "Tumble Bug."

Guy and Henry were real good friends, so they didn't have very much trouble negotiating a deal to lease. There was a railway on both ends of the property that was capable of hauling out boats of 65-feet in length.

Daniels Bros. Boat Yard Ft. Myers Fla.

Guye's first order was to build a 26-footer for a man from Miami. Harold, Guy's oldest son, was partners with him as the business started. So I decided to go over and help them out for a while.

Mr. Nate Hunt, who ordered the first boat, was a really nice person to be around. He had a big Norseman Yacht over on the east coast, and wanted this boat for a tender to go along with it. Mr. Hunt was a real tall, slender man, about 6' 6". He had Captain Drake, a very short man, about 5' 4". They were a real pair; both were fun to be around.

This was the first boat we built that was fiber glass covered, and it turned out really well. It was fast and a good performer. Mr. Hunt invited Guye to go along with him, and Captain Drake, to deliver the boat over to Miami. They went down around Cape Sable and up through the Keys. They fished along the way and really had a ball.

Later on, Harold decided to go to work for Gulf Life Insurance Co. In a few years Harold made "man of the year" agent for Gulf Life Insurance Co.

Over the next three years we built about five boats for local people, and had a lot of repair work.

Wilbur Storter was a local boat builder in Naples. He built a 55-footer for Mr. Briggs, the Briggs of Briggs and Stratton Motors, and was one of the chief stockholders of Outboard Marine Corp. Captain Frank Brown was captain of his yacht, the *Ungava*.

I remember when I was in Fort Myers, in about 1945; Mr. Briggs had a big sailing yacht named the *Sadie B*. Captain Frank was captain of her also. She was about 65 feet long. They sailed down through the islands all the way to South America taking pictures of birds. Mr. Briggs was a great photographer. Some of his pictures are still on display in the Naples Hospital.

Outboard Marine Corp. had a testing station in Naples that built experimental boats and tested outboard engines. I became friends with the foreman of the boat building department, Joe Chefneaux. Joe asked me how I would like to come over and help him build some boats. I talked it over with Guye and he told me it would be all right, and when things picked up, he would let me know, and I could come back if I wanted to.

Joe was a real good boat builder. He had worked at Miami Ship Building Corp. during the war, building PT Boats for the government. He taught me how to loft a boat from blueprints to full size. This I had never done before. All of the boat building I had done before was just by sighting everything. We would cut out the bow stem, keel, and transom, then set it up and put in a center spreader, wrap the two chine planks around it, and go from there.

We built a 40-foot catamaran for Ralph Evinrude. Ralph was a major stock holder in OMC, like Mr. Briggs. His father was the one they named Evinrude Outboards after.

After about a year Guye Daniels became busy, and wanted me to come back with him.

Along this time my second son was born. We named him John Collier after me and the Collier side of the family. He was born on Halloween so we nicknamed him "Boo." This name has stuck with him all through his lifetime.

Bruce Collier's oldest son, who was also called Bruce, had moved down to Naples to live with us. He had been working for Guye Daniels for a while when I was working at OMC. He had been trying to get on with OMC with me, so when I left, that left an opening for Bruce to get in. He was a real talented boy and learned the boat building trade fast.

After a few years with OMC, he went to work for Chris Craft over on the east coast, and from there he worked for Rybovitch.

Rybovitch at that time was the number one sport fishing boat in the country. Bruce went from there to Wellcraft, and wound up there top designer. He was really successful and put in a good financial position.

Bud Daniels had also come down from Fort Myers to work for Guye Daniels. Bud and I were real close, as I said before, he was like a brother I never had. He was Bill Daniels' son, who was Uncle Henry Daniels' son. Together, we built several plywood boats ranging in the 18 to 24 foot class.

Ted Martin, a sailing enthusiast, from Annapolis Maryland, hired us to build two sea gull class sailboats. After we built them, he donated them to the sea scouts. Then he decided we should build some racing class sailboats, as he knew Bud and I liked sailing. Bud had sailed with me up in Fort Myers when we were younger.

Ted brought a Southeaster sailboat design from Miami. Someone over there had designed and started a class for racing. They were 16 feet long and 5 feet wide. We built four of them. One was sold to a friend of mine Joel Benefield, and another to George Atkinson, who owned a drug store here. Bud decided he wanted one, and I bought one. These southeasters turned out to be very fast boats.

Another friend of mine, Andy Lorentzen, who was a coach and school teacher in Naples High School, had a 21 foot sailboat that he had built, called a Narasatuck, a Long Island design. We formed a sailing club and went to races in Miami, Fort Myers, and Sarasota.

I teamed up with Joel Benefield and we sailed in his boat in a one-of-a-kind race in Fort Myers Beach and got first place over all.

We went over to Miami to sail in the Nationals. The first day was pretty, with light breezes. That night a bad northwester came out, and we had about 25 or 30- knot winds for the next day. We started the race that day with 27 boats, and when we wound up, there were 13 of us left afloat. About half way through the race I told Joel we better forget about winning, and just try to stay afloat, to finish the race. I think everybody else had the same idea. We would see a boat ahead of us, and the next time you looked around, they would be dismasted or capsized. We came out fifth place for the two days. We were happy with this as we were new in the class.

Along about that time, my third son was born. We named him Michael David. He looked like the other two boys, except he had red curly hair.

Andy Lorentzen's Narasatuck

CHAPTER EIGHT

Fishing guides in Naples that I remember were: Joe Townsend, George Cole, Salvador Gomez, Major Regis, Johnny Combs, Jack Cannon, Preston Sawyer, Henry Earnshaw, Claud Forbes, Cecil Lamb, Durwood Salters, and Boo Davis.

Major John Regis was from London, England and was in the R A F in World War II. He flew Spitfire fighter planes and was shot down twice over London. After my mother moved to Naples from Fort Myers, she divorced Frank Marinelle, then married Major Regis. Major had a steel plate in his head from his airplane crashes. When he got in a bad mood we would tell him his steel plate had shifted. This got to be a laughing matter with the family and friends. Major was really a fine man, always doing my family a lot of favors.

He was a well educated man and had done a lot of traveling. His father owned mineral mines in Africa and he had sent Major down there to work and to learn mining. He had a lot of stories about the natives down there. After World War II, Major was on President Roosevelt's staff, here in the USA. His last boat was a 28-foot cabin cruiser built by Daniels Brothers in Fort Myers. People liked to go fishing with him, not only to catch fish, but to also listen to his tales.

Preston Sawyer and Jack Cannon were from Marco Island. Preston was born on Dismal Key, a little key between Marco and Everglades City. I think Jack was born on Marco or Henderson Creek. Preston also had a Daniels built boat, and Jack had a 40- foot Wilbur Storter boat.

Boo Davis and Durwood Salters came down here in 1925 from Davis, North Carolina, a little town near Morehead City. They went to work on the clam dredge. Boo told me when the clam dredge got to where it couldn't produce 500 bushels of clams a day, they shut down. Then Boo and Durwood moved to Marco and teamed up with Preston Sawyer, to go commercial fishing.

Then later on moving up to Naples and went into charter fishing.

Boo was a real character, and had several close calls on his life. He built his first charter boat, a 30-foot flat bottom. He soon sold it and bought a bigger one, it blew up on him, knocked him overboard, and the cabin landed on top of him. Some how Boo managed to swim out from under it to safety on the land. Later on he built a 10-foot flat bottom boat for duck hunting, with an outboard engine on it. It was a real fast little boat. Boo was going duck hunting down around Marco, and he was running down this creek that had a lot of curves in it, and lost control. The boat almost capsized, and threw him overboard, and then it turned around and ran over him. The propeller hit his arm above the elbow. It hit so hard it sheared the pin in the propeller, and almost cut his arm off. He managed to get back in the boat, but didn't have any extra sheer pins. With his arm almost cut off, he managed to tear one of the seats out. He had a pair of pliers and got one of the nails out of the seat, and used it for a shear pin. He got the motor started, and went back to where he had his truck and trailer parked, and drove to the Naples Hospital. He was almost dead from loss of blood but they sewed his arm up, and he was all right. As I am writing this, he is still alive, in his 90's.

Boo and Henry teamed up and built houses during the summertime, which was the off season for guiding. They would build a house or two during the summer and sell them, and then go back to guiding in the winter season. They were both very successful.

Henry Earnshaw disappeared years ago. He had a hunting camp down south of here, and they found his truck, but never found his body. Boo told me that Henry had terminal cancer and he was sure Henry had committed suicide. Why they never found his body is still a mystery. Boo says he thinks Henry went off from his truck, dug a hole and blew his brains out. Maybe gators ate his body. I guess we will never know for sure

Captain Cecil Lamb was from Fort Myers. He was in the Coast Guard during World War II, and after the war he wound up in Naples. He started out chartering a 26-foot Chris Craft named the *Silver King*. Captain Lamb stuck to chartering year around. The summers were slow for him but he made enough money in the season to tide him over through the summer.

Captain Lamb ran the Chris Craft for 20 years. Then he had Wilbur Storter build him a 30-foot cabin cruiser. While Wilbur was building this boat Captain Lamb told me he was building it to last as long as he would live, and it would be his last boat.

He was a tough man. When you booked him for a days fishing, you went, regardless of the weather. It didn't get too rough for him. During hurricane Donna, which was the worst hurricane in history to hit this area, Captain Lamb went down south of here, tied the Silver King up in a creek, and rode out the hurricane without any damage. He chartered up until he was 84 years old. He was right about his last boat, it out lasted him. Randy Wamble bought the *Silver King* from Captain Lamb just before he died and commercial fished with it for several years

Jack Cannon, Salvador Gomez, Johnny Combs, and Derwood Salter all died fairly young. George Cole was pretty old when he died. Claude Forbes retired and moved up to Lake Placid. The rest of the old bunch wound up captains of private boats, owned by the wealthy people of Port Royal.

Naples fishing guides

Marco Island had quite a few fishing guides. The ones I knew were Ralph Doxsee, his son Doyle, and his son in-law, Jackie Thompson, Ted Naftal, Nate Hunt, Johnny Stephens, and the Weeks boys, Johnny and Billy. Most of them had small open boats and specialized in tarpon, snook, and redfish. They were especially successful in catching snook on live bait. Nate Hunt Jr. was the son of the Nat Hunt, who I mentioned earlier, who I helped Guye Daniels build a boat for. Young Nate came into Guye's boatyard while I was working there and ordered a boat. It didn't ring a bell to me who he was, until I asked him if he was any kin to the older Nate, he replied, "I am only his son." Later on, when I started my fiberglass business, we built his son a boat, that made three generations that I had built boats for.

The Doxsess's, Jackie Thompson, and Ted Naftal, all bought boats from us. Ted wound up buying two boats, a 24' that he ran for several years, and then decided to go into a 31'twin diesel. Jackie stayed with his 24'for about 20 years. Doyle Doxsee died of cancer in his sixties, Ralph retired and he is now in his nineties. Johnny Stephens, Nate Hunt and Billy Weeks passed away earlier. Jackie, Ted, and Johnny Weeks are still running strong at this time.

Pappy Turner and his family played an important part in the early development of Naples. Pappy was originally from Morehead City North Carolina. He came to Naples around 1940 and bought a tract of land on Naples Bay. Pappy and his family were avid commercial fishermen and boat builders. He and his sons built the Big Dipper, and then the Little Dipper. The Fish House was opened in 1949. In addition to the boat building and fishing, the family was involved in dredging and hauling oyster shell and beach sand, which was important to the early construction of roads, and the first hospital in Naples. The family fish house and business became E. Turner and Sons, Inc. The family business continued to grow, although some of them pursued other interests. Pappy's oldest son, Archie, became Mayor of Naples from 1964-1968.

CHAPTER NINE

B enny Morris was a wealthy man from New York and Naples. He was always into building or remodeling houses and boats. He purchased some property on Harbor Island, Bahamas, and started building over there.

Already owner of 4 boats that I worked on several times, he then purchased an 18 foot fiberglass catamaran. Then he bought some outboard engines, and some other supplies to take to Harbor Island.

In the meantime, Jimmie Dunn had sold Gulf Coast Marine and bought a 72- foot yacht. He had been doing some charter work with her. Benny decided instead of shipping the supplies, he would charter Jim's yacht to carry them over, and take a few of his friends along for the trip.

He knew I had lived in Harbor Island and was familiar with the waters over there, so he asked me if I would like to go along as guide. Of course, I was always ready for a trip like this. I took a leave of absence from the boatyard and met the boat in Miami.

The next morning we pulled out to run across to Bimini, with the catamaran in tow. About an hour out of Miami there came up a little chop on the water. Jim didn't think it was bad at all, but Benny thought the catamaran was taking too much of a beating so we went back to Miami. He made arrangements to have her brought over on the freight boat. We headed on back for Bimini arriving there late that night.

The next day Benny decided the trip was going too slow, so he chartered a seaplane to fly him on over to Harbor Island, and told us he would see us over there.

We pulled out of Bimini, and ran across the Bahama banks and cleared Chub Key about dark. We decided to bypass Nassau and go right to Egg Island, around Spanish Wells, and into Harbor Island. The *Patricia*, that was the name of Jim's boat, made real good time for her size and power. She was 72-feet long and only about 14-feet wide, and had two 230 H. P. Detroit diesels in her. She cruised about 12 knots. We picked up Egg Island light just before daylight, went on around Spanish Wells, and into the lower harbor mouth at Harbor Island.

Benny had already built a dock on his property big enough to tie up the *Patricia*. That property is now Valentines Yacht Club. We unloaded our outboards and other equipment and stayed around for two or three days. Finally Benny decided it was time to leave. He was going to fly back to Miami and meet us there. It was blowing about 25 knots out of the east, and I told Jim it was going to be real rough going across the bar. He was drinking pretty bad then and he said it would be all right, so we got under way and started out through the harbor mouth. Jim had her at cruising speed. I didn't say anything. She went over the first sea and through the next one. It broke over her bow and came back through the pilot house windshield, and almost washed Jim off of the wheel. The *Patricia* was an old boat and you could feel her bending. I said, "Jim, you better slow her down or you are going to break her back."

Jim stepped back and said, "Here, you take her." I pulled the throttles back and slowed her down to about six knots, and then she was riding okay. About that time the German cook came running up to the pilot house and said, "We are sinking!" So Jim took over again and told me to go down and find out what was wrong. The galley was right up in the bow of the boat. When I got down there, water was about six inches deep on top of the floor. I finally got the hatch open to the bilge and it was dry. While I was kneeling down looking in the bilge, about a bucket full of water hit me in the back. I jumped up, looked up, and found out what was happening. The deck hatch wasn't dogged down and when she came down off of a sea, it would fly open and water would pour in. I reached up and fastened the hatch down, and that took care of that little problem.

The cook was really seasick. He laid down on one of the bunks in the crew quarters and wouldn't move. I tried to get him to come up in the pilot house, but he wouldn't budge. We decided to go into Nassau that night and rest up.

We were eleven hours making it to Nassau, which is about 65 miles. It was still blowing pretty hard when we got into Yacht Haven, but we tied up all right and spent the night there. The next day it calmed down, and we went on to Bimini, arriving there about 9 p.m. We tied up at Browns dock, that had a bar room and restaurant. Mr. Morris's guest had a good time dancing to the Bahama music, and we all had a good meal.

The next morning the weather was nice and we ran on over to Miami, got tied up and washed the boat down. Mr. Morris's guest rented a car and drove back to Naples. Jim and I drove his MG back.

Jim had another charter to the Bahamas in about a month, and wanted me to go with him, but we were busy at the boatyard and I couldn't get off. That was in 1960. On his return from that trip Jim decided to bring the *Patricia* back around to Naples. When he arrived at Marathon, hurricane Donna was approaching. The marina had emptied their fuel tanks in fear of an oil spill, and filled them with water so they wouldn't float off. Jim was out of fuel and couldn't go any farther. Hurricane Donna caught him at Faro Blanca Marina. The *Patricia* wrecked and sank. Jim swam to the light house tower at Faro Blanca; it was the dock masters office. It was a strong building, built as a replica of a light house, and he rode out the hurricane there. I guess I was lucky I missed that trip.

CHAPTER TEN

We knew hurricane Donna was coming a couple of days before it hit. It came up through the Bahamas and north of Cuba. A couple we knew, Gene Piate and his wife Kitty, and their two children, decided to ride it out at our house on Orchard Lane in East Naples. It was a new house and on high ground. Donna hit the Florida Keys and then turned north. I knew we were in for it then, because that morning the wind was 80 mph at 8 a.m. This was September, 1960.

I had Joe Benefield's southeaster sailboat in my back yard. I saw the boat rising up on the trailer about two or three inches, when the wind gust would hit. I had some cement blocks in the yard, so decided to put some of them inside of the boat to hold it down. About two hours later, the wind lifted the boat off the trailer breaking the hold down lines, and blew it about 100-feet in the air, and it landed about 100 yards away.

All the hurricanes I had been through before, we always had some friends over and had what we called a hurricane party. I could see this wasn't going to turn out to be a party. Elsie's youngest sister was visiting us from Harbor Island. That made a grand total of ten people and one dog. Sometime that morning another dog came up to the door, so we let him in, too.

The electric power went off about 9am, so we didn't have any way of knowing where the center of the hurricane was. About 11:30 it started calming down. By 12:00, it had calmed down completely. I thought this must be the eye of the hurricane. I turned on my car radio, and got a Sarasota station, that said the eye was about 100 miles south of there. We hadn't had any damage. Up until then the wind had been out of the east, and I knew when the eye went by, the wind would switch to the west and we would get the high tide. I decided to go down to the boatyard and get my tools. I knew when the tide came back in, the yard would be flooded.

Out on the road it was a mess— power lines down and a lot of tree limbs on the road—but I managed to make it down to the boatyard. It was wrecked. The roof was gone and everything else was in shambles. I got back to the house just in time. The wind had already started picking up again. By 1:30 it was back up to about 80 or 90 mph. At about 3:00, it sounded like a bomb went off on the roof. What was happening, the roofing was tearing loose from the plywood sheeting, and beating up and down on the roof and the water started pouring in. It seemed like you could see the wind, it was blowing so hard. Small pine trees would lay down flat on the ground when the gust would hit.

The wind had shifted to the west, and I remembered a story my granddad had told me about a hurricane they had at Marco, and there was 14 feet of water over Naples.

Our house was cement block construction and the walls were vibrating, and I knew it couldn't stand too much more of this. About that time we heard a loud explosion across the street and looked over, and saw the whole end blow out of a house just like ours. Luckily, the people had evacuated the day before.

The girls were almost hysterical. I was trying to keep calm but it was a job. Water was about six inches deep in the house from the rain, but the yard was still fairly dry, so I knew we weren't getting any flood waters yet. We were about three or four miles in from the gulf on fairly high ground. At about 4 p.m., it started calming down, and about 6 p.m., it had calmed down almost completely.

About that time a neighbor came running over and said his wife was having a baby. He couldn't get his car started and asked me if I could take her to the hospital. I told him I would try, so we started out. We got out on Tamiami Trail all right by moving a few trees off the road, and headed on in toward town. We got up to Airport Road, the trail was blocked by downed trees and power lines, so I went Airport Road north to Davis Blvd. It had about two feet of water on it, and getting deeper. My car finally drowned out and stopped.

The lady had a bag with her and she had some diapers in it. I took one of them out and dried off the wiring on the engine, and it started again. We made it about a quarter of a mile and the water was getting deeper all the time. It drowned out again. This time I couldn't get it started.

Some friends of mine came along in a swamp buggy and they told me they would take the lady on to the hospital. After an hour or two, I had the engine dried off, got it started again and made it back home.

The next day I started down to the boatyard and I stopped by my mother's place on Halderman Creek. Her house had blown off the foundation, and set back about four feet. Some of the windows were blown out and it was a mess.

A friend of mom's, Ralph Martin, a house mover from Fort Myers, heard about her house being off the foundation. He came down and offered to set it back up for her; she was thrilled.

When he finished the work, he and Mom were sitting at her table having a drink to celebrate. In walks Major Regis, and he was not happy, as he was very possessive of my mom. He didn't know Ralph was an old friend from years before.

Ralph could not pass up the chance for a bit of fun. The Major was getting very aggravated, and wanted him to leave. Ralph just sat back and said, "Why don't you just run along sonny boy?" Needless to say, Mom had to make both of them leave, with Ralph laughing, and Major very angry. Mom had two storms to deal with that week!

When I got to the boatyard it was in shambles. All of the boats we had in storage had floated off their blocks and were scattered everywhere. The good part was: I knew we didn't have to worry about work for a while. We didn't have any electric power or any outside communication for about a week.

The National Guard came in and we were under martial law for a while. It was a bad time for the insurance companies, but a good time for the working people of Naples.

CHAPTER ELEVEN

Elsie and I started having problems and she found somebody she liked better than me, so we wound up in a divorce. She took off for New York leaving me with the three boys. My mother was single at that time so she asked me to move back in with her, so I sold my house.

Mom's next door neighbors were a family from Georgia, the Sadlers. Mr. Sadler was in the lawn maintenance business and he had a daughter living with them. Her name was Rachel. She had two kids, a girl named *Sandra*, who was the same age as my youngest son Michael, and a younger son, named Robert. She had been married to a Marine and they were divorced. We started going together. She helped me with the boys quite a bit.

At this time, I met Captain Grant who was running a yacht for Mr. Fleishman, a millionaire here in Naples. Something happened and he sold his yacht, and Captain Grant got another job with a Mr. Powers, who had bought a 92-footer over in Miami. He was fixing her up as a charter yacht to run trips to Dry Tortugas.

Captain Grant asked me if I would like a job with him. Things were kind of slow at the boatyard, so I decided to go with him. We went over to Miami every Monday morning, worked on the boat all week, and then would come home for the weekend. This went on for two or three months and then Captain Grant decided he would retire. He was getting pretty old, and I guess he was getting tired of the responsibilities. I stayed on for about another month.

Mr. Powers was undecided whether to bring the *Lady Louise*, (that was the name of the boat), over to Naples or not. That was right along the time of the Russian Cuban missile crisis and he didn't think there would be many people wanting to go to Tortugas, being it was only 90 miles from Cuba. So I decided to quit and come back to Naples. My family needed me at home.

I carried the *Lady Louise* up to Miami Beach Boat Yard and left her there for Mr. Powers. He told me if things changed he would call me.

When I returned home to Naples, my friend Basil Symonette called me to come down to St. Thomas, V.I. He wanted to give me half of his business to come and help him. He owned a ships store and a marina, so I flew down and looked it over. I thought this could be a good thing. So I phoned Rachel, asked if she would marry me, and be willing to raise the 5 kids on St. Thomas. She said yes! My mom said no. She didn't want the boys to go. Rachel said she wouldn't marry me if I left my boys, and she certainly would not leave her two for anyone. So I told Basil I was not taking his deal and flew back home.

By then things had picked up at the boatyard and I went back to work for Guye Daniels.

Rachel and I decided to get married, and we bought a house in Coconut Grove, which was a new subdivision in East Naples. It was a real nice house, built right after hurricane Donna. Rachel was working at the Golfing Buccaneer as a waitress and making good money. With me working at the boatyard, we even had a little bit of money left over each week.

This friend of mine, Ralph Odom, had started chartering. He had a 26-foot Chris Craft that I had worked on at times for him. He asked me why I didn't go into the charter boat business with my knowledge of boating and fishing. So I thought I would give it a try. I had gotten my captain's license a year or two before, so all I needed was a boat.

With the help of my children, I built a 26-foot cabin cruiser in the back yard and bought a used Grey marine engine to put in her. I named her *Sandra*, after my daughter. We built it out of cypress framing and cedar planking. She worked out very well, fast and a great sea boat. I launched her right at the first of the season and got a slip at the Naples City Dock. We had a rewarding king mackerel season, and I found some real great customers that came back the next year.

I received a call from Mr. Powers that summer, and he wanted me to go back to work for him. I explained the situation. I had my own boat now, and was chartering, but would be glad to help him out when I could. He asked me if I knew anybody else who could work with us, and I thought of Vincent Marshall. He was a friend of mine that had been running a 46 foot Matthews Cruiser for a Mr. Balsh. He sold the boat and Vincent was out of a job, so I got Vince tied up with Mr. Powers. I figured between the two of us, we could handle it. The season was over and I didn't have much business for the summer.

Mr. Powers had the *Lady Louise* brought around from Miami, and tied her up at the Naples Yacht Club. There was still a lot of work to be done on her to get ready for the season. We finally finished up all we had to do.

Mr. Powers decided to make a shake down trip to the Dry Tortugas. The *Lady Louise* was a good boat for those trips, carrying a lot of fuel and fresh water. We carried a couple of Boston Whalers on deck that we launched with electric powered davits.

We fueled up and got out of Naples early in the morning. We ran 13 hours and hadn't picked up Tortugas, only making about 10 knots. I knew something was wrong because Tortugas was only 100 miles from Naples. I told Vince the compass must be off, and that we were west of Tortugas. The *Lady Louise* had an old radio direction finder on her that had been left when she was used by the Navy. Dave Trayer, a radio man in Naples who had adjusted our electronics, had showed me how to use the R.D.F.

There is a radio beacon at Loggerhead Key in Tortugas, so I beamed in on it, and it showed we were due west of Tortugas. We turned east and ran about two hours and picked up the light house at Loggerhead Key. It was pretty late at night when we finally got into the anchorage.

The next morning we launched the two whalers and went fishing. I couldn't believe how good the fishing was down there. We caught a lot of grouper, snapper and barracuda just trolling feathers and spoons.

We were tied up at the dock at the fort that night, so Mr. Powers thought it would be nice to have a barbecue. He had brought some steaks along, so we took our portable barbecue pit out, and grilled them for the whole party. The next day we were up early, had breakfast, and then went fishing again. We caught all the fish we wanted in just a few hours and had a fish fry on the boat.

The next morning we headed back for Naples, arriving safely back to the Yacht Club, and everybody was happy.

Mr. Powers went ahead and booked up the first charter. It was for four people, David Pabst and his wife of Pabst Beer Company, and Jim Colliopolious, and his wife. Jim was a local insurance salesman. They were real avid fishermen.

We left Naples about dark and ran down that night, so we could fish the next day. We had learned from our previous trip that the compass was off about 10 or 15 degrees, so we corrected for this and didn't have any problem finding Tortugas the next morning. I took Mrs. Colliopolious out the next morning on one of the whalers. We anchored up on top of this little rock bed, it was probably three or four feet deep, and started casting for snappers. I was looking down under the boat and saw a lot of lobsters, so I put on a pair of gloves, and went over board, and picked up 40 lobsters off that one little rock pile. We went on back to the boat and had a lobster feast.

After that trip we averaged a charter about every two weeks, and in-between, I was running my boat on day charters. We wound up the season with a trip to Boca Grande, tarpon fishing for several days. The summer was pretty slow. We made two or three trips to Tortugas with Mr. Powers and his friends.

At the beginning of the next season I had built up so much trade with my own boat, I decided to give up my job on the *Lady Louise* and go on my own. I told Mr. Powers and we parted still good friends. Vince Marshal's oldest son had just gotten out of the Navy, so Vince hired him on as mate, and that worked out real good for them.

Julie Colliopolious on the Lady Louise at Dry Tortugas

CHAPTER TWELVE

Frank Thornton was a commercial fisherman, one of the few successful ones. He was from Polk County, Florida, and started fishing up around Sarasota when he was 14 years old. Franks mother was a Smith, an old fishing family in that area. He came to Collier County in 1935 when he was about 15 years old. He made a trip to Kansas a few years later, and met his Dorothy, and they were married a little later in Everglades City, Florida.

Frank served in the US Coast Guard during World War II. He and Dorothy had three boys, Jim, Ray and Glen. They all grew up fishing with him. Dorothy delivered papers for the Miami Daily News when she wasn't cooking and keeping house. I met the family when I came to Naples and we became lifetime friends.

I helped Frank and the boys build a 30-foot plywood boat for mackerel fishing. Later on he contacted me and said he wanted to build a 58-footer, and wondered if I would help them design and build it. This sounded like a real challenge to me. Frank knew I had bought some cedar from a saw mill out in Pensacola. Rachel's brother, John Sadler, lived there and had a friend that owned a saw mill. We ordered 4,000 feet of white cedar from them.

The John's family had a saw mill in East Naples, where they sawed cypress and pine. We ordered pine for the bow stem and keel, and cypress for the framing. My uncles, the Daniels brothers, had sold out the boatyard in Fort Myers, and Uncle Frank had opened up a wholesale marine hardware store. I told Frank we could get all of our glue and fasteners from them.

We drew up a set of plans and started construction on Frank's property, on Davis Blvd. At that time they were on the outskirts of town. We got the stem, keel, and some of the frames set up. The county building inspector came along and told Frank we couldn't build that boat there. Frank told him that was his property, and he would build whatever he wanted to there. The best thing he could do was to get in his car, and go on down the road. Frank was a big strong man and meant business when he talked. The building inspector decided to take Franks advice, and left, and we didn't see him anymore.

Frank and his boys, besides being good fisherman, were good boat builders. He didn't spare any cost on building the *Lady T*. We used all epoxy glue and monel fasteners. Her frames were 2x6 cypress and we strip planked the hull with 11/4x2 cedar strips with epoxy glue in-between. When we finished planking her, we epoxy coated the whole inside of the hull. Her decks were 3/4 inch plywood fiberglass covered. Her first engines were 230 hp Detroit diesels. Later on, they re-powered her with a pair of 12V71 Detroits, they were about 1,000 hp each; a real fast boat with these engines.

The *Lady T* was launched in 1964, and turned out to be a fine boat.

Frank Thornton's 58' *Lady T.*

CHAPTER THIRTEEN

That next season was a real bonanza. I met this man from Arkansas, Mr. Hamilton, a road builder, spending the winter in Naples. The weather was real nice all winter, and the king fish were thick. Mr. Hamilton was chartering me three or four days a week and we would average 200 or 300 pounds of fish a day. I was able to sell the fish, as not many of the parties wanted more than two or three for themselves. With that money, along with my charter money, and the money that Rachel was making, things weren't too bad.

Mr. Hamilton stayed on until about the first of June. After the king fish had gone north, the grouper fishing was real good, and he loved to fish better than any one I had ever seen before. He was happy when the fish were biting. When they would quit biting, he would go down in the cabin to take a nap, and tell me to go on in to the dock when I got ready.

I picked up quite a few charters that summer after Mr. Hamilton left. He said he had to go back to Arkansas and build some more roads, so he could come back next winter and go fishing. That next November he showed up again.

After we made a few trips, one day he said, "John, we need a bigger boat. Why don't I buy one and let you charter it, when I don't want to go out."

This seemed like a good idea so I went along with it. At that time, there were not a lot of used boats around, so we decided to go over to Fort Lauderdale and look around.

There was a big boat dealer over there called Rodi Chris Craft. We found a 30- foot Chris Craft Sea Skiff, with twin 185 hp engines. She was rigged for fishing with a fly bridge and outriggers. We really didn't need all that on this coast, but they looked good anyway. Mr. Hamilton made them an offer, they accepted, he gave them a check and he owned the boat.

We drove back to Naples, and the next day to get Dan Skinner and his wife Arletha, to drive us to pick up the boat. I took Rachel with me for the trip back. We finally got ready and got under way around 10:00 that morning. We went down the Intracostal Waterway to Miami, through Biscayne Bay, then down through the Florida Keys. When we got up to Everglades City, it was about dark, so we decided to put in there for the night. Mr. Hamilton rented one of the cottages at the Rod and Gun Club. We spent the night and ran on up to Naples the next day.

After Guye Daniels sold out, Bud Daniels and Henry Happ leased the Gulf Coast Marine. They had some boat slips so we rented one from them. I was already running my 26-footer out of there, so it worked out pretty good. Mr. Hamilton named his boat *Marty Ann*, after his daughter.

After about three or four months the first Cuban exodus started. The Cubans over here were buying every boat they could, to go over to Cuba and bring back their families. They came around and wanted to buy the *Sandra* from me. I saw it was going to be a problem running two boats, so I decided to let her go. They offered me $3,000 which, at that time, was a fair price for a 26-foot boat. They fueled her up, and put two 55 gal drums in the cockpit, and went straight down to Cuba, and brought back 18 people. When they came back they took the *Sandra* up the Miami River. About a month later they called me and asked me if I wanted to buy the *Sandra* back. I told them I couldn't pay them back as much as they had paid me for her. They asked me what I would give them, and I told them I only had $1,600, and they accepted it.

Rachel drove my oldest son Paul and myself over to Miami and we brought her back. I had several people run her that season, and finally Bill Parker, an old friend of mine, decided he would like to run her. I had plenty of charters booked up and Bill was good at catching kingfish. This worked out real well. Bill took right over and it made it a lot easier for me on the *Marty Ann*.

I remember this one charter. This lady was sitting on the companion seat across from the helmsman seat. She was watching her husband fishing, so she was turned around backward in the seat, with her feet up against the bulkhead. I told her not to push so hard because she might tear the seat loose from the cabin side. I had this fancy tackle box I had borrowed from Bud Daniels, I kept under the seat. She got excited and gave a hard push; the seat came loose and flipped over. Her head hit the tackle box, dead center, and it flew open, scattering hooks and fishing lures all over the cockpit floor. Her feet were in the air and her head was in the tackle box. I jumped down off the pilot seat and helped her up, and seeing she wasn't hurt I started picking up fishing tackle.

Everybody got a big laugh out of this. Rachel was with me that day and she said it looked like I wasn't interested in the lady, as I was picking up fishing tackle and Bud's tackle box.

The rest of the season went along pretty good until about June. Mr. Hamilton started having his family down and I would have to cancel my charter parties. This put me in a real mental strain, but I couldn't blame him for wanting his family to come down and fish either.

I had a talk with Mr. Hamilton and he under stood, so I went back to running my own boat. Bud Daniels had become good friends with Mr. Hamilton and he and Henry Happ had decided to get out of the boat repair business, so Bud went to work for Mr. Hamilton full time. They decided not to charter the *Marty Ann* any more. Mr. Hamilton had a real bad heart and Bud helped him out a lot. Bud was a good fisherman and Mr. Hamilton loved to fish, so this worked out real well.

Bud had never been married. At this time Rachel was working at the Fish House dining room. Sandy McCormick was also a waitress there. Sandy's sister Helen came to work fresh out of a divorce, with three children to take care of. She worked there several months, getting more discouraged at trying to work and raise three kids. One night she came in about in tears, and told Rachel she wished she could find some "old mullet" that loved kids, who would marry her and help her out. (Helen called all of us fishermen, old mullets) Rachel stood there watching Helen in her sadness and Bud popped in her mind. She called me and told me to bring Bud by her girl friends house. Fifteen minutes after they met, they took off together. From then on they were inseparable. Needless to say, there were wedding bells soon after that.

Hansen Chris Craft Sales of Fort Myers and Sarasota bought out the lease on the boatyard and all of the boat slips. Bob Martin was one of the salesmen there. He had taken in a 37-foot Colonial Cruiser at that time. I knew by this time, to be successful in the charter boat business, I was going to have to have a larger boat. I made a deal with Bob to buy the Colonial. Bill Parker had been running the "*Sandra*," and wanted to buy her, so I let him have her. I named my new boat *Sandra*, too. She worked out real well. She was big enough that I could carry a party of six and not be crowded. We made it through the summer all right, and the next season was a real good one.

Most of the old time guides had dropped out, or had gotten jobs on private boats. Captain Lamb was still running strong. Ralph Odum was still running, along with Major Regis, and Preston Sawyer. They all liked me so they sent me all of their over flow, and I was real busy. I ran 62 trips with out a day off that season.

As I started out one day, this lady was right beside me asking all kinds of questions. She saw the crab pot buoys and asked me what they were. So I explained to her that a line ran down to a wooden trap that had and opening in it. The crabs would go in the small funnel shaped opening, and couldn't get back out, and the crabbers would pull them up, open the lid and get the crabs out, once a week. She asked me if they did this year around. I told her there was a closed season for about six months in the summer.

She asked me, "What the crabs do when they close the season?" I told her most of them had gone north in trucks. I had a holder over on the side of the cabin beside the steering console; it had a round hole for a coke, or beer can, and rectangular hole for a pack of cigarettes. I didn't smoke, so I carried a can of 3 in1 oil in it, to oil my reels. She saw this and asked me why I carried an oil can where my cigarettes were supposed to be. I was getting pretty tired of answering questions, so I told her that sometimes I had to talk so much I had to oil my jaws. She took the hint and went over and sat down.

My boys were a great help to me during my charter boat days. One of them would usually run with me as mate, and when we got in after a charter, the other three would come down and clean the boat from stem to stern.

One of my best customers was a man from Orlando, Mr. White. He would come down every Saturday and go grouper fishing. He was in the automobile upholstery business. He would bring a big box with him, we would fill it with grouper and ice them down, and he would carry them back to Orlando. I asked him what he did with all the fish. He told me he gave them away to his customers for advertisement. It was better than running ads in the newspaper.

Mr. White had only one leg and he told me one time he got in a fight with a man with one arm. I bet that was a sight to watch.

I had this one charter with four men that wanted to go grouper fishing, and we headed out to the grouper banks. They were drinking beer when we left the dock. We got out to the banks and had a nice catch and started in. We ran about thirty minutes and I started looking around and only saw three men. I asked one of them what happened to the fourth man he said, "Oh, he fell overboard about fifteen minutes ago."

I turned around and started back and he told me not to go back, that he was a good swimmer and would make it all right. We were still out of sight of land, so I ran back and found him swimming along. He told me he was all right, and for us to go on in and he would swim ashore,

He told one of the other men to throw him his hat. We finally got him back in the boat and ran on in to the dock.

The next couple of years the fishing started declining. The kingfish were getting scarce and we had to run farther off shore. I think the over fishing of them in the Florida Keys was the main problem. Kingfish are a migratory fish. They would spend the summer months up in the northern gulf and start their winter migration in November. They would pass by Naples in late November, or early December, when the gulf water temperature got to around 70 degrees. If the weather got too cold, they would go on south and spend the rest of the winter in the Keys. We had a couple of cold winters, so the fall run wasn't too good.

They start their return north around the first of March, and if the weather got too hot too soon, they would go right on by, and we would only have a few weeks of fishing. This didn't really bother my business too bad because I had built up such a good local trade. The people would go with me anyway even if the fishing wasn't too good. The only thing wrong was: I didn't have the fish to sell, and this was cutting into my finances pretty bad. On a good day of king fishing I would have about $100 dollars worth of fish to sell, plus my charter money.

Around 1970, Major Regis decided he would retire from chartering. He had this customer from Rochester, New York he had been carrying fishing for several years, and he asked me if I would be interested in taking him. He told me Mr. Clark was a real good man and good pay, so I told Major I would be glad to take him. He was about 55 years old at that time, married and had three kids, one boy and two daughters. Mr. Clark was an alcoholic at that time, but you couldn't tell he drank to be around him. He was a secret drinker. We fished that season. He and his family probably went out ten or twelve trips. They were real nice people. When the fishing was bad, they didn't seem to get upset.

Mr. Clark's father had loaned George Eastman money to help start Eastman Kodak Company. Around 1900 Eastman couldn't pay Mr. Clark back, so he gave him like one thousand shares of stock in Eastman Kodak, and Mr. Clark had inherited this. Money was no problem with him.

My last charter boat, *Sea Foam*.

At the end of the season, Mr. Clark told me he was going to buy his own boat, and he would like for me to run it for him, if I was interested. I was getting discouraged with the charter business and knowing Mr. Clark like I did, I told him I would like that. He asked me how much money I would need. He told me it might not be a full time job, but he wanted me to take care of the boat he bought, and to go fishing once or twice a week when he was in Naples. He asked me how much money I needed and I told him, and he said that was no problem.

After Major Regis quit chartering he had gone to work for Hansen Chris Craft Sales as a part time salesman. I wasn't aware of it at the time, but Major had sold Mr. Clark a 40 — foot Chris Craft Sport Fisherman. Around March of that year, Mr. Clark asked me to drive him out to the airport to catch a plane home. His family had left earlier. I drove him out to the airport and shook hands and he told me he would see me next year. He didn't mention any more about the boat or job. I drove on back home not thinking much more about it.

When the first of the month came up I got a check for $800.00. I went down to Hansen Chris Craft and Major told me about the boat. Mr. Clark told him to tell me to rig the boat like I thought it should be rigged for fishing. This came as a shock to me, but I was glad. I thought it might be a good time in my life to have a little security. I went ahead and sold the *Sandra*, but kept a couple of my local jobs that I had, carrying people out on their own boats once a week. I thought I would keep them through the summer until Mr. Clark got back, and I saw what my situation was going to be with him.

I spent most of that summer around Hansen Chris Craft rigging up Mr. Clark's new boat. She was a nice boat. She had V berths right up in the bow, and behind was a state room on the port side, and opposite that, on the starboard side, was a head and shower. The galley was up in the salon, and a couch that pulled out and made a double bed. She had a fly bridge with dual controls. The only bad feature was she had gasoline engines. I knew she wouldn't have a very long cruising range but we could live with this.

Mr. Clark came down around Christmas, we had the boat ready to go, and he was really impressed with it. He named it, *Maradon*, after himself and his wife. His first name was Donald, and her name was Mary. Their daughter Sarah Lynn was the oldest, and married to Doctor Mark Moliver. They lived in Baltimore Maryland. He worked at John Hopkins in Baltimore. Richardson was next; he wasn't married at this time. And then there was Memi, the youngest. She wasn't married either.

That winter was a real good season. Our first trip with the *Maradon* was to Marathon, in the Florida Keys. One of the Clarks friends, a Mr. Baker and his wife, had a 40-foot sport fishing boat, so they accompanied us down to Marathon. Their captain was Elija Love, a friend of mine. We had pretty weather going down, but that night, a norwester came out and it was blowing about 25 knots the next morning. Mr. Clark had rented a cabin at Faro Blanca, at the marina we were staying in. Mary and son Rick, with his English girlfriend, Jilly had come down with us. They all came down to the boat that morning, and Rick and Jilly were itching to go fishing. Mr. Clark and Mary said it was too rough for them, and the Bakers backed out too.

Down in the Keys, when the wind is out of the north, in the Gulf Stream, if you don't get out too far, it usually isn't too rough. I told Rick and Jilly we could try it if it was all right with Mr. Clark. He told us to go ahead. I think he really wanted to go, too, but because of Mary he decided to stay with her at Faro Blanca.

We got out to the edge of the Gulf Stream, and it was pretty rough, about 6 to 8-foot seas, but the *Maradon* was riding it pretty well. Rick and Jill were good sports. I rigged a couple of trolling lines and put them out, and went up on the fly bridge. We hadn't been trolling but about an hour when Rick called out, "I've got a sail fish." I turned around and saw him jump. I kept trolling along slow, and Rick reeled him in pretty quick. I put on a pair of gloves, grabbed him by the bill, and dragged him over in the cockpit. He was about 7 feet long. That was my first sailfish. Rick said we might as well go on in, that was enough for him for one day. We arrived back at the dock before noon. The Clarks and Bakers came down to the dock and couldn't believe their eyes. This really put a feather in my cap. From then on the Clarks thought I was the world's greatest fisherman.

The next day the wind switched around to the north east and we ran on back to Naples. We followed up the shore line and it was pretty nice. We did a lot of fishing that year in spite of the weather. I was glad I wasn't chartering, because of the weather and the declining fishing.

Mr. Clark and Rick heard me talk about Tortugas so much; they asked me if we could take a trip down there. I told them sure we could go, the only drawback was the gasoline situation, but we could go by way of Key West and fuel up there. That was all right with them, in fact, Mr. Clark suggested we go to Marathon, follow the key down to Key West, and across to Tortugas, as we weren't in any hurry anyway.

We waited until June to go to Tortugas because the weather is so much better in the summer time down there. Mr. Clark, Rick and Jilly went along, and I took my youngest son Bob. We got down to Tortugas without any mishaps. We trolled around the reefs that first day and caught all the fish we needed to eat. That afternoon we anchored up just south of the fort, at the ranger station. Just before dark we decided to put bait out for tarpon. In just a few minutes we had a big one on. I reached over the side to gaff him, trying to get him right in the mouth, so I wouldn't kill him. I missed and got him right in the throat and the blood ran everywhere. Pretty soon the rangers came out to see what all the blood in the water was. I told them we caught a tarpon and released him, and I thought the sharks had caught him. We ran on back to Key West the next day and spent the night at the Key West Yacht Club.

The next day we started up to Marathon on the Atlantic side. About five miles out of Key West, one of the motors ran away. I turned it off and went down in the engine room and found we had wrung off one of the propeller shafts right behind the engine coupling. We went on to Marathon to Baliff's Boat Yard on one engine. It was on the weekend and they couldn't haul us out, but Mr. Baliff said he could get us a diver. The diver came right on down. We had a spare shaft on board and had it in by dark. The next day we ran on back up to Naples.

CHAPTER FOURTEEN

Mr. Clark asked me how I would like to spend the summer on the Chesapeake Bay with the boat. I told him that sounded good to me. He said he was going to spend about a month at Hopkins Clinic in Baltimore, and he would like to have the boat up there. We decided on Annapolis as a good place to base out of. He told me I could take the family and he would rent us an apartment to stay in. He gave me $4,000 in cash, and asked if I thought that would get us there. He said he didn't believe in credit cards, as he made his money off interest, and he didn't intend to spend it that way.

I talked it over with Rachel and she was ready to go, so I asked the kids. Sandy and Bob said they would like to go, but Boo and Mike said they had rather spend the summer at home. Rachel's mother said she would stay with them so we were all set to go. Paul was in the Air Force. We left Naples early one morning and ran to Indian Town Marina, a little town between Lake Okeechobee and Stewart on the east coast. The next day we made it to Cocoa Beach, and stopped at a marina to fuel up. I jumped off the boat and ran on into the ships store to find the dock master. Rachel and the children decided to go to the ships store also. She stepped off the boat and started past the fuel pumps, and got a frightening surprise. This large, white goose was standing between the pumps, we thought casually observing us, came at her with a vengeance! His feathers were ruffled, and the noise he made was awful. She jumped back on the boat, pushed the kids into the cabin. The dock master came out and asked what happened. She said, "Mr., you must not want any business, having something like that mean goose here."

He laughed and said, "He only lets one person get off a boat."

She said, "Mr. you need to have your goose cooked."

The next day we got to Fernandina Beach. Rachel had a cousin, Griggs Turner, who lived there, so she called him and he and his wife and daughter came down to the boat. He worked in the paper mill there. We asked them if they would like to ride up to Brunswick, Georgia the next day. Griggs said he and his daughter would ride up with us, and his wife could drive and pick them up. They really enjoyed the trip, so after we let them off we ran up to Isle of Hope, Georgia, a little town just south of Savannah. It is a pretty area with oak trees. The whole trip through the Georgia Intracoastal is pretty—big saw grass flats and winding rivers. There aren't a lot of towns or docks along the banks and you can make good time. The next day we made it to Charleston, South Carolina, and tied up at the city marina.

Our oldest son Paul was stationed at Charleston Air Force Base. He was married at that time, we called them, and they came down to the marina. We spent the next day in Charleston riding around with them.

The next day we made it to South Port, North Carolina, that had real nice marina and a good restaurant. The next day we made it to Morehead City, North Carolina. We docked at the city marina and found it to be a real friendly place. The next day we made it to Hoboken Bridge, North Carolina. I fueled up and spent the night there.

The next morning we got under way, and everything went along smooth, until we got into the Pamlico Sound, and then both motors stopped. The first thing I thought about was water in the gasoline. I opened up the engine hatches and started draining the fuel filters. They were both full of water. We had gotten a bad batch of fuel at Hoboken. I drained the filters and carburetors and finally got her started again, and got under way. We would run about an hour, and I would go down and drain the filters again until finally we got rid of most of the water, or I thought we had.

We finally made it to Coinjock, North Carolina and spent the night there. The next day we made it to Norfolk, Virginia. We decided to go into Willoby Bay Marina, at the south end of the Chesapeake Bay. A real bad summer squall came up and there was already a lot of smoke and haze. Visibility was just about zero. Every time a bolt of lightning would flash, I could get a bearing on the marina. We finally got up to the sea wall, and a young man came out into the rain and helped us get tied up. He said the basin was full and we would have to lie out there, if we wanted dockage. After we tied up, the young man started walking away. I gave Bob a ten dollar bill and told him to run and give it to him, for helping us get tied up. Bob caught up to him, and handed him the ten. The boy turned around and said he just got a cancellation from another boat that was supposed to show up, and we could have his slip inside the basin.

The next day we ran on up to Annapolis, and had a hard time finding dockage. We finally found a slip at Sorrell's Boat Yard. It was even harder finding an apartment to stay in. We finally found one on the fifth floor of a condo, right beside Trumpy's Boat Yard. Sorrell's Boat Yard was up Spa Creek, with a bridge between it and the bay. This was a real challenge getting through this bridge, as there was always ten or fifteen boats waiting to go through, and about that many cars waiting to go over it. The bridge tender would open it, let about ten boats through, and by then there would be about 25 or 30 cars backed up, and he would close it, and the same thing would happen to the boats. It usually took about 30 minutes to get through.

After we had been in Annapolis about a week, Mr. Clark came down and wanted to go fishing. He read in the newspaper where someone caught some blue fish off Love Point. I looked on the chart and found the spot, across the bay and a little father north. I rigged a couple of trolling lines and we ran over to Love Point, and had real good luck. We caught about 15-20 blue fish in the 8 to 10 pound class. We brought them back to the boatyard and Ben Sorrell, the owner, and his dad were glad to get the fresh fish.

Ben had a son about the same age as our Bob. We all became real good friends. When we came back to the Chesapeake later on, Ben always found dockage for us. We stayed in Annapolis about two months, fishing about twice a week.

Mr. Clark decided we would go out to Ocean City Maryland, so we moved out of the apartment and back on the boat, and took off for Ocean City. We ran up the Chesapeake to the C and D Canal and went through it, into Delaware Bay, and down to Lewes, Delaware. We spent the night there.

I found out a strange thing about that coast. At Lewes, Delaware, there is about an 8 or 9 foot tide, and about 30 miles south at Ocean City, there is only about 18 inches of tide. It seems unreal that two places that close together could have that much tide difference.

We got into Ocean City, and it was a real busy place. We stayed at a place called Ships Café, a marina motel combo. Mr. Clark and a friend of his showed up a couple days later and we decided to go fishing. You had to run about 50 miles off shore there to catch tuna and big game fish. We had an early start, but it was blowing pretty hard. We ran about 25 miles and it kept getting worse. Bob was down below with Mr. Clark and his friend and I was on the fly bridge. Mr. Clark sent Bob up, and he told me Mr. Clark said, turn back, if the boat didn't break in two, he would. He fell down and stuck his foot through the air conditioner grate. So I turned around and started back in.

We decided to put out a couple lines as we couldn't run fast anyway.

As soon as we got the lines out we had on a couple fish. They were really giving us a good fight. They turned out to be big blue fish in the 15 to 20 pound class. We caught several of them before getting in.

That afternoon, Mr. Clark and his friend packed up and left. He had to get back to Rochester and he told us we could go ahead and start home.

The next day it blew about 30 knots, so we decided to lie over. The next day it calmed down and the forecast called for a northeaster to come out. We decided to get started, and ran about five hours, and a heavy fog set in. There was no wind, but there was a big swell running. I was running to a buoy down off the Virginia coast. I ran my time out and I couldn't see a thing. We didn't have any kind of sophisticated navigation equipment, but I did have a radio direction finder. I stopped the engines to hear if we were near the bell buoy, but instead of the bell, we heard surf breaking. With a closer look at the chart, I saw a couple of shoals that had about 20 feet of water over them. These swells were so big they were breaking on these shoals. Then I knew where we were. In a heavy fog like this, you seem to loose all sense of direction. I knew when we got down off Norfolk, Virginia, I would be able to pick up the radio beacon at Norfolk and run in on that beam. In a couple of hours the fog had lifted, and we could see where we were. We ran on into Norfolk and spent the night at Willoby Bay Marina, again, it was a real nice marina with good accommodations.

The next day we started down the Intracostal Waterway. We arrived in Charleston, South Carolina about three days later, and spent two or three days with Paul and his wife. They were still stationed at the Air Force Base.

Hatteras Yachts had just come out with their 53-foot sport fisherman at that time, and they had a demonstrator in Charleston. Mr. Clark had mentioned before about a larger boat, so, I looked her over pretty close in case he was serious. She had a pair of 500 hp Detroit diesels, carried 1,000 gallons of fuel, and 250 gallons of water. This would be ideal for Tortugas trips and the runs up north he liked to make.

We left Charleston and got down to Stewart, Florida without any major difficulties, and started across the Intracostal Waterway. When we got over to the St. Lucy Locks, they asked us how far we were going. I told him we were going all the way across. He told me that lightning had struck the bridge at Port Mayaca, they couldn't raise it, and it would be a week before they got it fixed. We decided we could make it home in two days by going around the end of Florida. We ran back to Stewart and down to West Palm Beach that night.

The next day we were in the Florida Keys, and that night was so beautiful, we just decided to anchor up instead of going into a marina. It felt good to be back in the peaceful Florida waters again. The next day we were back in Naples.

Mr. Clark came down early that year just before Christmas and, just as I suspected, started talking about a bigger boat. I told him if he wanted to make trips like we had been doing, it sure would be handy to have a diesel-powered boat with more cruising range. We should not be worried about fuel all the time. He asked me if I had any ideas about what boat we should get, I told him about the 53 Hatteras Sport Fisherman that I had seen in Charleston, South Carolina.

He pulled out his check book and wrote out a check for $50,000, told me to order one, and ask if they would take the Chris Craft in on trade. I went to Tom Bundy, manager of Hansen Chris Craft and Hatteras, and he told me they would be glad to take the old *Maradon* in on trade. He filled out the papers and I took them to Mr. Clark, and he signed them.

We made several short trips that season on the Chris Craft, while waiting for the new Hatteras, up to Captiva, down to Everglades City, and quite a bit of fishing. The weather was pretty bad that season, and I was glad I wasn't chartering. The fishing had really declined almost to an unbelievable stage. The king fish runs were over and the grouper had really been thinned out.

One morning, I cranked the engines for a warm up and noticed one of them went way up on the temperature. I began looking around and found the heat exchanger tank had split open, and all the fresh water was running out. I told Mr. Clark what had happened, and said it was a good thing we had her traded in.

He said, "No, John, that isn't the way we do business, let's get it fixed, because we want to turn this boat over to them in good condition."

That was the kind of man Mr. Clark was. He was the most compassionate man I had ever known and completely honest. He trusted me beyond belief. I had my own checking account at the bank for boat expense and trips, and he never let the balance get low. I wouldn't have stolen a dime from this man if my life depended on it.

He promised Mary, his wife, if he bought this new boat he would quit drinking, and to the best of my knowledge he kept his word. Around the end of winter, he asked me when the best time of year was to catch tarpon at Boca Grande. I told him I thought May, June and July were about the best months. He told me to make arrangements there for a week dockage, and hire a local guide if I thought it necessary.

Captain Buck Lee ran a 57-foot North Carolina sport fishing boat that belonged to Avondale Mills out of Alabama, who was a good friend of mine. He did the fishing circuit every year, winding up in Boca Grande for about two months. He told me to contact Jimmy Mobley, who had docks for rent. I had heard of Jimmy before, so I called him and made reservations for the first week in July.

When the time came to go to Boca Grande, Mr. Clark couldn't make it. He had to get back to Rochester for something and he told me to take his friends and go ahead. They rented a place in the Gasparilla Inn to stay, so I had the whole boat to myself at night. I hired Thomas Knight to be our guide. You really need local knowledge in Boca Grande Pass if you want to catch fish, and it had been about 15 years since I fished there. We fished at daylight and dark and caught tarpon every day for the whole week we were there.

CHAPTER FIFTEEN

Tom Bundy asked me if I would like to run a 44-foot Hatteras up to Chicago. Mr. Clark had told me earlier, when I took the job with him, that when he wasn't using the boat, it was no use me hanging around. Go ahead and do what I wanted to do. So I told Tom I would be glad to make that trip for him.

The boat belonged to a news reporter in Chicago. He said he would meet me in New Orleans, and go up the Mississippi with me. Rachel had a brother that lived in Gulf Breeze, Florida; a little town just across the bay from Pensacola. She said she would ride that far with me.

We started early one morning, and by about 3 pm we were off St. Petersburg. I had noticed a vibration on one of the props, and it had seemed to have gotten worse in the last hour or two. I stopped both engines and put on my swim suit and jumped over board to examine the props and shafts. I rolled the prop that seemed to be vibrating and noticed it was turning crooked. On closer inspection, I found the shaft was cracked right behind the strut. I got back on board, cranked up the other engine, and got under way again on one engine. We were right off the entrance into Clearwater, so I decided to go in there to the Clearwater boatyard to have her hauled out.

As I entered the boatlift, a sudden squall came up. I had to crank up the other engine in order to maneuver into the slip where the travel lift was. As soon as I put it in reverse, the shaft finished breaking off and I lost the prop. The next morning we hauled her out and a diver went overboard to look for the prop I had lost. He looked for about an hour without any luck. He said there was about two feet of silt on the bottom and the prop was down under this somewhere.

I told the manager of the yard to go ahead and order another prop and shaft, as we were in a hurry to continue on to Gulf Breeze. I called Mr. Smith, the owner of the boat, and told him what happened, and he was upset.

They were about three days getting the shaft and propeller installed. I had talked quite a bit with the manager of the yard while we were there, and I noticed he was a brother Mason. When he gave me the bill for the repair, I called Mr. Smith with the amount, and he said he would mail a check right away.

The yard manager said to me that they didn't usually let a boat go without the bill being paid. He knew we were in a hurry to get going, and on the strength of me being a brother Mason; he would let us go ahead. I told him I would call him back to be sure he got his money from Mr. Smith, and if he didn't, I would pay him.

We ran on up to Cedar Keys, spent the night, the next day ran across the gulf to Carabelle, spent the night there and fueled up. The next day we made it to Pensacola Beach. Rachel's brother came down and picked us up and took us to his house in Gulf Breeze. The next morning, I left by myself and ran up the Intracostal Waterway, into Lake Pontchartrain, to the New Orleans Yacht Club, to meet Mr. Smith.

The next day he and I got an early start, entering the Interacostal into the Mississippi river, and up to Baton Rouge, Louisiana. There are a lot of tugboats and barges on the Mississippi.

We had to fuel up in Baton Rouge, and this turned out to be a real project. The fuel barge was right on the banks of the river. It had a big iron over hang on it that caught the Hatteras about 6 inches above the guard rail. While we were fueling up a big wake from a tugboat came crashing in, and broke off two of the stanchions that hold up the hand rail on the Hatteras. While we were discussing where to tie up for the night, one of the crew members off a tugboat over heard us talking, and said we could lay along side their tug, just down river from where we were. He said they had some good fenders and we would be safe there. We ran on down there and tied up along side. The tugs on that river are big, from 80 to 125 feet long. They were continuously going by with big tows, and there is continually a big wake and wheel wash from them. The tug we tied to, had a big generator that ran all night, and you could hear it roar for about a half mile away. Needless to say, we didn't get much sleep that night.

The next day we made it up to Vicksburg, Mississippi, into a little canal off the main river. Some barges tied up along the shore line and we tied up along side them. Three or four days later we made it up to Memphis, Tennessee to a Yacht Club that had some real nice docks.

The reason for taking the Hatteras to Chicago was to sell her. Mr. Smith had a friend at Memphis that was a yacht broker, and he came down to the boat, and asked if the boat was still for sale, and if it was, he had a buyer for it. Mr. Smith told me he hated to disappoint me by not finishing the trip to Chicago. I didn't tell him, but I was real happy to get the whole deal over with! I had enough navigating on the mighty Mississippi for a life time. I had heard a lot of stories about it, now I knew they were true. Mr. Smith paid me and bought my airline ticket back to Miami. I called Rachel, she met me in Miami, and we drove back to Naples.

CHAPTER SIXTEEN

Mr. Clark's 53' Hatteras was finally ready, and Tom Bundy asked if I wanted to go to New Bern, North Carolina, pick her up, and bring her back to Naples, so they could finish outfitting her. This sounded good to me, so they flew Rachel and me up to New Bern.

The plant manager was Brudge Hopkins. He and his wife took Rachel and me out to dinner that night. I found out that he was a friend of Bill Kepler, my friend I had sailed with years ago.

The next morning we started south with the 53 footer, and made it down to Myrtle Beach, South Carolina, and tied up at a marina. She had twin Detroit diesels and I went down to check them. When I pulled the oil stick out of the port engine, it was full right up to the top of the oil tube. I smelled it, and it was about 90% diesel fuel, instead of oil. I pumped 14 gallons of fuel and oil out of it, and re-filled her with the proper amount of oil. I called Tom Bundy in Naples and told him what happened. He told me to try to get her to Charleston, South Carolina, even if I had to run on one engine.

Under way, the next morning, I watched the oil pressure and everything seemed all right. We arrived into Charleston early that afternoon; a Detroit Diesel mechanic was already there at the city marina, working on another boat. I explained to him our problem and he seemed to know what was wrong. He pulled off the valve covers, and he was right. It was a loose injector line, pumping raw fuel right into the oil chamber and on into the base of the engine. The mechanic had his tools with him and had it fixed in a few minutes.

The next morning everything went along all right until we got down to Savannah, Georgia. I slowed down to pass a shrimp boat as we entered the Savannah River. Rachel looked back and said: "We are on fire!" Smoke was boiling out the exhaust pipes. I checked the instruments and everything seemed to be normal, so I ran down and checked the engine room. There wasn't anything on fire in there, so I picked up speed, and the smoke cleared up. We pulled into Thunderbolt,

Georgia and when I slowed down, the smoke came back. After tying up, I found another Detroit mechanic, working on another boat. It seemed like we were lucky finding mechanics when we needed them. He had me crank the engine, so he could see what color the smoke was, and determine whether it was fuel or oil burning. He said it was oil smoke, so that was not good news.

But the good news was, Morgan Engine Company was in Savannah, and they were the ones that sold Detroit diesels to Hatteras Yacht Corporation. They went right to work tearing the engine down to see what was wrong.

It was December the 18th and we were trying to get home for Christmas. Rachel's mother wasn't doing too well at home. We called Boo, our #2 son, to drive up and bring Bob and his cousin Kenny Sadler, to finish the trip up with me when they got the engine fixed, and take Rachel back home with him.

They were only three days overhauling the engine. It had broken a wrist pin in one of the pistons, but it didn't let go. It spread out and scored the cylinder walls and that was letting the oil burn and causing all the smoke. They told me to take it easy for a couple of days and it should be all right to run her as hard as I wanted to.

I enjoyed our stay in Savannah. It is a beautiful town with a lot of history behind it. The next morning we got under way in a heavy fog. We were picking our way from one channel marker to the next, when I saw a tugboat coming up behind us, pushing a barge. I noticed he had radar, so I dropped in behind him and followed him for about 30 miles. Then the fog lifted so we could start running again. We got all the way down to Daytona Beach, Florida that night.

The next morning, we got under way and everything went along smoothly until we got down to Fort Pierce. I hit some kind of submerged object and bent one of the props, but could still maintain about 17 knots with out too much vibration. We got down to Stewart and started across the canal to Lake Okeechobee, then hit something else. This time she was really shaking, so I decided to go back to Stewart, get her hauled out, and change props.

When I reversed to turn around, a big palmetto log came floating to the surface. It had hung up on one of the propeller blades, and when I reversed that engine, it threw it off. I breathed a sigh of relief and headed on out. We made it to Indian Town that night, about 10 miles from Lake Okeechobee. I called Mr. Clark and told him where we were, and it looked like we would be home for Christmas. The next day we made it on into Naples.

I turned the boat over to Hansen Hatteras Sales. They had to outfit it with outriggers, bow pulpit, a 13 foot Boston Whaler that we carried on the forward deck, and a few more odds and ends.

Mr. Clark came down about a month later and the boat was ready to go. He told me he had Mr. Williams, a CPA that used to work for him and some lawyer friends of his, and he would like to take them around to Golden Beach, a suburb of Miami Beach. Mr. Clark told me to hire a mate for the trip. Jim Hutchison worked around on different boats, and I had met him some years before. I asked him if he would like to come along, he said he would love to.

Mr. Williams was blind, an older man in his sixties. The two lawyers were younger men. We loaded up with supplies and got started. Our first day, we ran down to Everglades City and spent the night there. The next day, Mr. Clark chartered a boat to take them fishing. He hired Dinks Bogess, who was an old timer in the area. They had a good time with Dinks and caught a lot of fish. I fried fish for the party that night and we all had a good time.

Mr. Clark said he would like to run down to Plantation Key, which was about half way to Miami. I told Jim we would have some fun with these young lawyers. We started on down the coast following the shore line down to Cape Sable, and I headed on down the old yacht channel to Lower Matacombe Key. After you leave Cape Sable and Sand Key, which is just south of the Cape, you are out of sight of land for a little while.

Jim was on the bridge with me, and after we had been running about two hours, the two lawyers came up on the bridge. I had just sighted Lower Matacombe Key. I told Jim, where the two lawyers could hear me, that it looked like Key West we were approaching, and it seemed we were way off course. I saw the lawyers look at each other, and I knew we hooked them.

Mr. Clark had told me earlier to stop and get some shrimp, to fish before we got into Plantation Key. As we pulled in to the dock, I called down to the dock master, and asked him if this was Key West. He called back and said, "That is close enough." That really confirmed our little joke. We got some shrimp and headed on up for Plantation Key arriving about 3 o'clock. I pulled out of the channel and anchored up under the lee of another little key to do some fishing. We were all down in the fishing cockpit, casting with spinning rods. Mr. Williams, in spite of being blind, could cast with a spinning rod really well. I told Jim to go get the field glasses, and look around to see if he could figure out where we were. Jim started looking around, and said it looked like Plantation Key, just to the east but he wasn't sure.

We fished for a couple hours and then went on in to Plantation Yacht Harbor, which had a real good restaurant at the marina. That night, Mr. Clark took us to dinner, and as we were all sitting around the table, Mr. Williams said, "You boys sure had some fun with a bunch of green horns, didn't you?" He knew what was going on all the time. We all got a big laugh out of it.

The next day we ran on up to Golden Beach. Mr. Williams had a friend who had a house on the water, and a nice dock to tie up to. We spent three or four days there. Mr. Williams and his lawyer friends stayed there, and Mr. Clark, Jim and I brought the boat back around to Naples. This 53 Hatteras was a fine boat. She would cruise at 20 knots easy and was good in a head sea.

Later on that season, Rick and Jill came down with her brother and his girlfriend from England. They wanted to go to the Tortugas. The weather hadn't been very good, so I told them we could go down to Marathon and see how it looked, then, if it wasn't too bad , we could go on to Tortugas from there. We could follow the Keys down to Key West, and then over to the Marquisa Keys, and then across to Tortugas.

The next morning the wind was out of the northwest at about 20 knots and it was raining, but they were anxious to go, so we started out. We ran down the intercostals to Coon Key and followed the shore line down to Cape Sable. I knew if we stayed in shallow water, the seas wouldn't be as big; we could make better time. From Cape Sable we ran across to Marathon, and went into Faro Blanca Marina.

That night the wind switched around to the east, and was blowing 25-40 knots. Rick was anxious to get to Tortugas, so I told him we could at least get to the Marquisa Keys, as the wind was right behind us and it wouldn't be too bad. We got down to the Marquisas about noon and decided to go on across the Rebecca channel to Tortugas. I slowed down to about 12 knots. The seas were about 10 foot, but we made it in good shape. We got into the anchorage at Fort Jefferson, and there was a big mooring buoy in the middle of the anchorage that the Coast Guard had put there for their use. When they weren't there anyone could use it, so we tied up to it for the night.

During the night the wind shifted around to the south, at about 25 knots, it was too rough to do any fishing. We decided to go in to the dock and tie up so they could go explore the fort. Fort Jefferson is an interesting place. The walls are red brick, 8 feet thick. It was a federal prison during the Civil War, and the largest fort in the Western

Hemisphere. Dr. Mudd was imprisoned there. He was the one that doctored John Wilkes Booth, who shot Abraham Lincoln. While he was in prison they had a bad epidemic of yellow fever, and Dr. Mudd found a cure for it, and they pardoned him. One of the cells still has a sign over it that reads: "Dr. Mudd's cell."

The next day it calmed down, but they forecast another northwester for the next day. I told Rick we better make a run for it while we had a chance. They were disappointed but they went along with my decision. We made several cruises and fishing trips that year. Mr. Clark asked me if I would like to make another trip up to the Chesapeake Bay, and spend the summer up there. I said, "We have a lot better boat to go in now."

CHAPTER SEVENTEEN

We pulled out of Naples in May, for one of our trips up the east coast, with Mr. Clark and his son on board. I hired Jim Hutchison to go along as mate. The day we left there was a hurricane brewing down in the lower Gulf of Mexico, but it wasn't near enough to cause any problem yet. We left Naples about daylight, and arrived in Stuart about dark. The next day it was raining, but we decided to go anyway. Listening to the weather report, I learned that the hurricane was moving north, and was about the same latitude we were on, except it was on the opposite side of the state. It was causing a lot of rain all the way across the state. We made it up to Daytona Beach that night. It was really miserable running in the rain, the curtains and the Bimini top on the fly bridge leaked, and Jim and I stayed wet all the time. Plus, we couldn't see very well.

We got into Daytona and Mr. Clark thought we better lay over for a day or two, and see if the hurricane would go on by, and the rain would slack off. We stayed the next day, and the day after that it had quit raining, so we started out again. We got to Savannah, Georgia that night, and it was still raining. We heard the hurricane had turned into a tropical depression and was still heading north up through Georgia, causing a lot of flooding. The next day was fairly clear, so we started on up the Intracostal Waterway.

We ran about two hours and came across a big Norseman Sport Fishing boat that had gotten out of the channel, and ran aground. I asked Mr. Clark if we could pull him off and he agreed. I ran the bow of the *Maradon* out as close to the bow of the other boat as I could without running aground, and Jim threw them a line. I reversed and backed out towards the channel, and swung the other boat around so he would be facing the channel. As I turned him around, we quit moving. The man on the bow called back to someone, and asked if the motors were running. They started the engines, and with them running, we were able to pull them off. He came right in behind, and followed us to Charleston, South Carolina.

We went on to George Town, South Carolina, and had dockage right between a paper mill and a steel mill. It was really not a nice odor there! The next day we ran up to Morehead City, North Carolina.

During the whole time we were going north on the *Maradon* my family became very concerned about the hurricane weather we were in. Mrs. Clark had called Rachel from Rochester, New York because she could not contact us, and Rachel told her she couldn't get any response either.

Before leaving I had given Rachel a telephone number for the ship to shore "Marine" operator, in case of an emergency, She called that number and was given a number to call in North Carolina, and one for Virginia Beach. The TV was talking that a lot of power lines were down up the East Coast and she had an idea it could be why she hadn't heard from me.

Rachel called the North Carolina number thinking that was the area I would be near. The operator answered, Rachel asked for the ship to shore "marine"operator.

The girl said, "What base do you want, Ma'am? And what is the Marine's name you want to talk to?"

Rachel explained she was trying to talk ship to shore, and explained about us traveling through the waterway there. She said if you would put your marine operator on, she would know what I am talking about.

The girl put her supervisor on, and she said, "Ma'am, we have two Marine bases in this area so we need to know what base, and what Marine."

Rachel became so upset she said, "I don't want a base, and I for sure don't want a Marine; I've been married to one of those, all I want is to talk to a Yacht going up your waterway, with these call numbers."

The operator threatens to have Rachel arrested.

Rachel hung up and called our Marine operator in Naples back.

She thought Rachel may be just too upset also, so she called the same numbers herself, got the same answers Rachel did, and called Rachel back laughing so hard she could hardly talk. She said, "I did not believe anything you said Mrs. Morgan, but I sure do now." She finally contacted a ship in the area I was in, and it reported back that we were fine.

When Rachel called Mrs. Clark and told her we were OK, then, told her about the operators, she became so upset at them she wanted their numbers, to get them fired.

Rachel said, "If I can calm down and laugh about this, you can too."

It was still very rough from the hurricane that had gone through. So we decided to stay in the Intracoastal Waterway and up the Pamlico Sound. It started raining, and rained all the way to Coinjock, North Carolina.

The next day we launched the Boston whaler, and I took Rick out fresh water fishing. We caught a couple small bass and that was about it.

We ran on up to Norfolk VA., then on into Willoughby Bay Yacht Basin, to spend the night.

Windmill Point is right at the mouth of the Rappahannock River, with a beautiful marina, two restaurants, and apartments you could rent. Mr. Clark had a boat slip and apartment rented, so that he and Mary, and whoever else was there, did not have to stay on the boat. After we had been there a week or two, Jim flew back to Naples, and Rick flew back to California.

Mr. Clark decided I needed some help on the boat, so we hired a local boy, Jim, home from college for the summer. He had done some boating around that area, and had quite a bit of knowledge of the area. We did quite a bit of cruising around the Chesapeake, and fishing, catching quite a few blue fish.

We decided to run down to Norfolk, and go out into the Atlantic, to do some offshore fishing. We headed on down to Willoughby Bay to spend the night. The next morning we got up early, and ran 50 miles southeast, offshore. As we started to troll, I sighted a fuel tank floating around. It may have been ejected from an airplane, probably a trainer from a base in that area. We trolled over toward it, and saw a lot of dolphin swimming around. We circled around it, and caught several dolphins, and some king mackerel. Then after a couple more hours trolling, we decided to reel up and run on in.

We had been under way only a few minutes with Jim running the boat from the fly bridge. I was down below when he called me to get up there.

He slowed down, and said, "Look under the boat."

There were thousands of fish! They looked like blue fish. I ran down below and we put out a couple trolling lines, and immediately we had on two! It turned out to be yellow fin tuna in the 15-20 lb. class. We circled around there till we filled the fish box. Mr. Clark asked me what we were going to do with all those fish. I told him we wouldn't have any trouble getting rid of them when we got into the dock.

On the way in from that trip, I was listening to the ship to shore radio, and heard Johnny Downing on the *Miss Budweiser* calling. He was and old friend of mine from Boca Grande. They were fishing out of Virginia Beach. It was good to talk to some one from "down south." I had no idea they were in that area too. The *Miss Budweiser* was a 53 foot Rybovitch sport fisherman, a beautiful boat, belonging to the Budweiser Beer Co.

We returned to Willoughby Bay and as we tied up, people flocked around to see what we had caught. I started throwing fish out on the dock and people were grabbing them up! We made lots of friends that day! This one lady standing on the dock, watching all this, asked me where we caught all these fish. I told her we were offshore. She told me her husband ran a party boat, but she never saw fish like that! Later, I learned that they just fished in the bay and didn't go offshore.

We left for Windmill Point the next day. After cruising around the bay area for about a month, Mr. Clark decided he and Mary would go up to Baltimore, Maryland where their daughter lived and spend a few days with her and her family, and then go on back home to Rochester. So the next day we took them up to Baltimore in the boat, and I couldn't find any dockage there. Mr. Clark asked me if I had any ideas. I told him I would call an old friend of mine in Annapolis, Ben Sorrels, to see if we could tie up there for a few days. Ben was glad to hear from me and told me to come on down, and he would make room for us. We ran in and spent the night there. The next day the Clarks left to go back to Rochester.

I then called Rachel to come up and meet me at Windmill Point, to ride back with me. Our number two son, Boo, drove her up along with our daughter Sandi, and friend Susan. Mike, son number three, rode as far as Charleston, and stayed with our oldest son Paul, to be picked up on the boat with us, on the way back. After I spent the night at Sorrels in Annapolis and changed oil in the boat, I left for Windmill Point. Rachel and the rest were waiting on the dock for me as we arrived. We spent the night there and left the next morning for home.

When we left we made it all the way to Oregan Inlet North Carolina. There were a lot of charter boats working out of that marina, around a hundred or so. It was kind of a quaint place, the docks were old but all we needed for the night. Some old man came out to help us get tied up, and told me to, "Tie her up good cause it's going to blow tonight." Some of the charter boat captains came down and started talking to us.

They saw Sandi and Susan in their bikini, and I think that got their interest up! One of them told me to take his pickup, and take my family over to the beach. The people in that part of the country are real friendly, acting as if they had known you all their life, and are ready to help you, if you need anything. We rode over to the beach, then back to the docks. There was a big restaurant and bar, and we had dinner while the captains were having their beer and a good time.

The old man that told me to tie her up good was right, it blew hard! About 25 or 30 knots all night! The next morning, one of the mates off one of the charter boats was singing a song, "Geraldine, got your Dramamine." I think he was still hung over from the night before.

It was still blowing hard. Most of those boys are real sailors, so bad weather don't mean much to them, they run offshore anyway. They came to ask me to move my boat, as her bow was sticking out in the canal, and they couldn't get past. Most of their boats were in the 30 to 40 foot class, and that was what the docks were built for. I told him we were ready to leave anyway, and would pull out. He helped us untie and then went off singing his song, "Geraldine, got your Dramamine." Rachel said this didn't sound too good to her.

There were two ways to get south, down through Pamlico Sound, or the Intracoastal Waterway. The Pamlico Sound is the shortest, so I choose that route, even though it was still blowing about 25 knots out of the south. I had always heard about how rough the sound got, and this day, I found out for myself! I couldn't believe it got this rough as shallow as it was! We had to slow down to about 8 knots; the seas were real steep and close together. Everything in the boat that was loose was upside down or wet! I had to run like this for about 9 hours, and finally got to the south end of the sound. With the seas smaller, I was able to get up to cruising speed, and run to Morehead City, North Carolina.

Morehead City is a friendly place, and there is a lot of activity around the city Yacht Basin. We were in for a real treat! One of the scallop boats came in and the captian came over and said, "Bring your buckets for as many scallops as you want, I'm not going to sell mine tonight." I could not believe it, when I saw what I thought would have been a lot to me, he said it wasn't enough to bother with. We scooped up a large bucket full and he tried to give us more!

The next day we ran to Southport, North Carolina to spend the night. The next day we made it to Charleston, South Carolina where Paul lived, and where Boo had left Mike to ride on home with us on the boat. We spent a couple days with Paul and his wife, then, headed out for Naples. The rest of the trip was really nice, but uneventful.

CHAPTER EIGHTEEN

About July, Rick and Jill came down and wanted to go to the Bahamas. My mate Jim Hutchison couldn't go. Paul, my oldest son, just got out of the Air Force in Charleston, decided to take a couple of weeks to go with me. He had started working at a service station as mechanic, with no future there anyway.

I contacted Dewey Garguilo, an old friend of mine, who owned Naples Tomato Growers, and owned a couple of Yachts. He was a member of two private clubs, Cat Cay Club, and Chub Cay Club in the Bahamas. I knew they were nice places to go. Dewey had told me earlier that if the Clarks ever wanted to go, he would get us passes; we could stay there and use their facilities.

Charley Knowler was running a 46 foot Egg Harbor Yacht for the Harrington's, friends of the Clarks. They were real nice people and wanted to know if they could go along in company with us. I told them we would be glad for them to come along. We ran down to Ocean Reef Club, in the Keys to spend the night, and the next morning, run on over to Cat Cay, from there over to Chub Key. The diving and fishing are a lot better at Chub than Cat Cay; the harbor is land locked, so that makes it a nice place to be. There is a winding channel cut into this large harbor.

Charley and his people decided to go over to Nassau, so we parted company there. My party fished a couple of days out of Chub Cay, and then we ran on over to Little Harbor Cay. We spent a couple days there, diving and fishing, then started home. Pulling into port in Miami to clear customs, the inspectors started questioning me about one of my passengers. "Who is that aboard your yacht? He doesn't seem to fit in your crowd."

I laughed and told him, "He is only the owner's son." Rick was in his favorite outfit, Hawaiian shirt and ragged cut off jeans, and lots of bushy hair.

"Ok, proceed, Captain."

We continued on to Naples.

After five years with the 53 Sport Fisherman, the Clarks decided they wanted a more suitable boat for just yachting. They had become very active in the Yacht Club in Naples, and had been looking at the 58 Hatteras Yacht Fisherman. They asked me what I thought about it, and I told him it was an excellent choice. Mr. Clarke and I went to Hansen Chris Craft and Hatteras sales in Naples, and traded in the 53, for a 58-footer.

My son Robert, and I, flew up to the Hatteras factory in New Bern, North Carolina, and brought the 58 down after it was built. We had a slip at Hansens, so when we returned, I spent several weeks decking it out. Mrs. Clark had an interior decorator for the inside. It shaped up beautifully in no time at all.

Our shake down trip was to Faro Blanca, on Marathon in the Florida Keys. My son Boo went along as mate.

On the return trip, about half way home we met with a norwester. That was a real shake down. The tide was to low to go up the Intracoastal at Coon Key, so we had to go out around Cape Roman. Seas breaking over the bow, coming back and hitting the windshield, then water started coming out of the electronics box, then over the helmsman station. We knew we had more work to do on the boat. It performed well, except for the leaks.

The Naples Yacht Club gathered people for a caravan of yachts to cruise to Marathon. Mr. Clark was appointed "Cruise Captain," so we were to lead the fleet. He was thrilled to receive this position, and told me that he was happy that he had me to captain him. My son Paul was mate for me.

We only stayed in Marathon one night and then cruised down the Atlantic Ocean side to Key West, to Ocean Side Marina.

That night, after everyone had left their yachts for a night out, we captains met to go out. Captain Charley Knowler, Captain Bud Daniels, myself, and Paul took off, and wound up at Sloppy Joes bar. While sitting there having our drinks, a girl came over and sat on Pauls lap, and asked him to go home with her. She asked which one of us was his dad, and Bud Daniels said he was. Paul sat there dumb founded, red as a beet and not saying a word! We sure had a laugh with all that!

Leaving Key West through the N.W. channel, it was blowing hard out of the east. We decided rather than head straight for Naples, to follow the shore line and come inside at Coon Key, Intracoastal to Naples.

One of the last outstanding trips for the Clarks was a cruise on the boat up to Disney World. I had Jim Hutchison as mate. We stopped at

Rio Mara Yacht Club at Vero Beach for them to visit friends there, and spend the night, then on up the Intracoastal Waterway to Jacksonville. The next day we went into the St. Johns River, down to Palatka. That night it was a hard freeze. The bird bath, on the lawn at the Holiday Inn where we tied up for the night was frozen solid. We ran on down to Sanford Yacht Basin, for them to go to Disney. We were there about 5 days, and then headed back for home. Back in Naples, they flew home to Rochester, New York.

Mr. Clark's 53 foot Hatteras

CHAPTER NINETEEN

I became restless, and was thinking heavy about boat building again. So I decided to make a mold, and build a boat out of fiberglass. I designed a 24 x 9-1/2 wooden plug.

Rachel said no to fiberglass in our back yard, the wooden ones were bad enough! So I rented a place in a warehouse and set up shop.

I knew the fishermen in this area didn't have an adequate boat for fishing inside the bay, and outside in the gulf, so the one I designed would work for both.

Word got out, and I sold about five boats before I could build my own. Some of the fishermen wanted just hulls, or partial finished, so they could afford one, and finish on their own as they could.

The first customer was Captain Ralph Doxsee, a Marco fishing guide, saying that's just what he needed. He just wanted a hull to finish himself, the way he wanted it. I decided then to sell to any stage of completion, no two look alike, and no two cost the same. Orders for these custom built boats came pouring in!

I had asked Ralph, since he got the first one, to call me for the trial run. When he called, we launched her at Marco and took her into Marco Bay. A large boat went by pulling a big wake, so I gave her full throttle, and hit the wake at full speed. Ralph ducked down behind the console as we went through the wake, and then came up smiling. With that smile, I knew I had a winner with that 24 footer! No spray inside the boat, so we were all happy!

So from renting a small bay in the industrial park near the airport, I had to expand fast and rent several more bays. That was the beginning of Morgan Boats of Naples, Inc. My four sons, and two of my brother-in-laws, and several of my nephews, came right on in to help out. We expanded so quickly I wound up buying the whole building. It was a very profitable business, the beginning was great! The rest is another whole story in it's own self!

When Mr. Clark got down that season, I told him what I had done. It looked like I was going to have to leave him. I felt obligated to my family to create work for them. He said he understood my situation, and asked me if I would be willing to finish out the season. That would make 10 years we had been together, and I agreed. They weren't using the boat much anyway. We stayed good friends up until his death a couple years later.

CHAPTER TWENTY

As I mentioned, my buddy, George Messer, who lived close to me when we were growing up in Fort Myers, and I stayed friends through the years. He went off to the Navy, for 20 years, and I went off to the sea, on every boat I could! After the Navy, he and his wife Lila and children lived in Palatka, Florida, and he retired as a deputy sheriff there.

Coming in from a charter fishing trip one day, Rachel and I were pulling up in the driveway, and she said, "John, who is that man sitting on the porch? He looks like he's sitting there asleep."

As we got out of the car, I realized it was George! After long years of not seeing him, it was great for him to be back. He stayed about 4 days, and we enjoyed talking over "good times."

A year went by without hearing from him, but again, there he was sitting on the porch when we drove up. This happened again each year.

Being tired of charter boating, along about that time, I had taken the job on the 53 foot Hatteras for Mr. Clark. I had to take it to Fort Lauderdale for some work on it. Since Rachel and I had not had time to ever go on a honeymoon, we decided she would go with me to bring the boat back to Naples. Her mother came to stay with our children. Bags were packed, and at the door.

"Here comes George!" Rachel said. "George, I wish you would have let us know you were coming. John and I are leaving."

He asked, "Where are you going?"

She told him we were calling this our honeymoon, as we never had one, but we would be back in about 3 days.

George said, "I always wanted to make that trip around the end of Florida. I think I will go with you."

Rachel about fainted, but gave in to his going along. He really enjoyed our honeymoon.

Our children just loved George; they thought he was so funny. He would always sit on the floor, between the coffee table and the couch. He would hold his head back and close his eyes, just sitting there, arms on the table and couch. Our youngest son Bob and his wife Frannie came over one evening and she said, "George, why do you sit like that on the floor and your head back and eyes closed?"

George just smiled at her and said, "Frannie, I'm praying for you."

She said, "Oh that's nice, keep it up."

Rachel asked him didn't he want to sprawl out on the couch, and his answer broke our hearts. "I have to tell you now, I have cancer, and I've already gone 2 years over the time they gave me to live. They gave me 5 years, and I've already lived 7 years. I have fulfilled all my dreams but one. I have always wanted to go on a trip to the Bahamas with John!"

Rachel said, "George, would you be up to it if you got the chance?"

He said, "I believe the Lord will give me the strength."

Rachel looked at me, and I said, "George I have a 30 foot Morgan sailboat in the back yard, get on board."

He and I sailed for Bimini the next morning. We spent the night there and then sailed on to Chub Cay, then on to Nassau. When we arrived, I called my ex sister-in-law Ruth and she picked us up to go for dinner at her house. We spent an extra day there sightseeing.

That night, I was sleeping forward on the V berths and George was on a bunk in the stern, and just before daylight, George yelled out, "There's somebody on the boat!" I jumped up and immediately found out my trousers were missing, that I had rolled up with my wallet in them, right at my head. We ran down the dock for help, and passing the telephone booth, there lay my trousers! No wallet in my trousers, but then I saw it on the floor, no money but everything else was there.

We left there and set sail for Cat Cay, got to N.W. channel light just before dark, and I heard an SOS from a power boat that had lost his engine. By this time it was getting pretty dark. He gave me his loran reading, and I located him right away. He said his engine broke and his boat was leaking. I asked would he settle to be towed to Cat Cay where we were going. He was more than happy to do so. I ran my engine and sailed all night, getting into Cat Cay about noon. We left him there, and sailed away for Naples.

When we arrived back in Naples, George told me how grateful he was that I had taken him on his dream of a lifetime trip. It was so sad when he left that time, as it seemed we all knew that was his last trip down to see us.

A short time after that, his daughter called to say George was in the Gainesville Veterans hospital and wanted to see me. I left right away to get there, and he was so happy. He wanted to ask me if I would be a pall bearer when he passed on. My answer was yes. I came back home the next day. He passed away about a week after that. I went up, and fulfilled my promise. His family was so happy to know I kept my word to him. I miss George, even now.

Young and care free, the wind on his back, is the way he grew up. He never had time to "be still." His love of the outdoors is obvious in his younger years, and has never changed in his retirement years.

John took life as it came, and always made the best of it, under any circumstances. He has chosen the pleasant times and the families that loved him and helped him through the years after his father passed on, they understood his restless spirit, and all know it runs deep in him.

To meet him and hear his slow southern drawl, you think, how "easygoing."

He has chosen to eliminate the tragedies and accentuate the positives.

The first boat built by "Morgan Boats of Naples"
A 24 foot open fisherman

From the beginning of John's life to his retirement years, all you will find are friends and boats. If he has ever met you he considers you a friend. Any waterway or boat that he has been around or on is part of him. He made this his way.

380716